MW00584010

March 11, 2022

Dear Ford,

This book, or one like it
has been on my bedside
table for almost 70 years.
It was compiled a woman
who thought that she
would not live to
raise her children.

Its quotes from the
Bible and literature
for inspiration.

I hope that you
read from it from
time to time and
it means something
to you. I love you!

Beby

SOMETHING TO LIVE BY

To Our
Aunt Sis:
We love it and thought
you would also, dear.
God Bless You,
Joanne, Don
Rick, Dana
Pam, Bob and
Lil' Bobby

December 25, 1967

SOMETHING
TO LIVE BY

Collected and Annotated by
Dorothea S. Kopplin

Doubleday & Company, Inc.
Garden City, New York

To
EDWIN

To the authors of poems quoted in this book:

I assembled this material from memory so, when the demand came to have it printed, it necessitated a detailed search through all I had read since childhood to locate the quotations and give proper credit. With neither titles nor author's names to work from the task was exceedingly difficult. After working on the book for six years I spent an additional three years trying to identify each selection. Many of them I was unable to locate. I trust the authors will understand my efforts and have sufficient sympathy with the purpose of the book, to accept any omissions.

I wish to thank all those who aided me in the preparation of this book and the authors and publishers, listed in the table of identification, who so graciously permitted use of their creations.

Dorothea S. Kopplin.

PREFACE

When I was told I could not live to bring up my children I decided to write a book to serve as a substitute in their lives. The task was to bridge the gap in education not filled by church or school, and to do so in a way that would develop individuals with ability and desire to find happiness and contentment in life.

A first step toward such happiness, it seemed to me, was to learn to appreciate something of real permanence in life beyond and above the material things; a deep love of nature would do just that. To feel a sense of kinship with nature and thence the Universe, gives strength and confidence that belittle material losses and worldly ambitions.

Fortitude and courage are further essential elements of character for fine living; and finally, a realization of the power and joy to be found in a true sense of the spiritual.

To leave a chart or blueprint for guiding and teaching such a way of life I decided to talk to them in terms of thoughts from literature which I had found true and helpful in life.

To My Son

Do you know that your soul is of my soul such part
That you seem to be fibre and core of my heart?
None other can pain me as you, son, can do;
None other can please me or praise me as you.
Remember the world will be quick with its blame
If shadow or stain ever darken your name.
Like Mother, Like Son, is the saying so true
The world will judge largely of Mother by you.
Be this then your task, if task it shall be,
To force this proud world to do homage to me.
Be sure it will say, when its verdict you've won,
She reaps as she sowed. This man is her son.[a]

A pilgrim, going a lone highway
Came at evening, cold and gray
To a chasm, deep and vast and wide.
The old man crossed in the twilight dim.
The chasm held no fears for him
But he paused when he reached the other side
And built a bridge to span the tide.
"Old man," said a fellow pilgrim near,
"Why waste your time in building here?
Your journey ends with the close of day
You never again will pass this way.
You've crossed the chasm deep and wide
Why build ye here at eventide?"
The pilgrim raised his old gray head,
"My friend, in the path I've come," he said.
"There followeth after me today
A fair haired youth who must pass this way.
The chasm which held no fears for me
To the fair haired youth may a pitfall be.
He, too, must cross in the twilight dim.
My friend, I am building this bridge for him."[b]

CONTENTS

1 WHAT IS HAPPINESS?

Do you want to be happy? You can be!
We sometimes miss the great joys in life by snatching too
eagerly at the false and glittering froth. Anyone can earn
happiness; oftentimes it is close at hand yet unseen.
To find happiness, we must search our own hearts, for it
comes from within, through our own efforts and beliefs.

"The fount of happiness is in the heart."

In this search for happiness one must constantly remember:

Naught's had, all's spent—where our desire is got WITH-
OUT CONTENT.[1]

The secret of happiness is not in doing what one likes, but
in liking what one has to do.[2]

He who harbors a slight will miss the haven of happiness.[3]

Each unit of nature has its special work to do and each per-
forms its function to perfection in accordance with the laws
of the universe. So also human beings, each has a distinct
contribution to make. Be what you were intended to be. Give
what you OUGHT to give:

If you can't be a pine on the top of the hill
   Be a scrub in the valley—but be
The *best* little scrub by the side of the rill;
   Be a bush if you can't be a tree.

We can't *all* be captains, we've got to be crew,
   There's something for all of us here.
There's big work to do and there's lesser to do.
   And *the task we must do is the* NEAR.

If you can't be a highway then just be a trail,
   If you can't be the sun be a star;
It *isn't in size* that you win or you fail—
   BE THE BEST of *whatever you are.*[4]

"WE LOOK TOO HIGH FOR THINGS CLOSE BY."[5]

Happiness is WHERE IT IS FOUND, and seldom where it is sought.[6]

Some people have every reason to be happy but they insist on thinking they are unhappy. Those who persist in feeling abused close the door to happiness when they might easily enjoy its richness.

   You have to *believe in* happiness,
   Or happiness never comes.
   I know that the bird chirps none the less,
   When all that he finds is crumbs.

   You have to believe that winds will blow,
   Believe in the grass, the days of snow;
   Ah, that's the reason the bird can sing:
   On his darkest day he *believes in spring.*

You have to believe in happiness,
It isn't an outward thing:
The spring never makes the song, I guess,
As much as the song makes the spring.

Aye, man's heart could find content,
If it saw the joy on the road it went,
The joy ahead when it had to grieve,
For the *joy is there*—but *you have to* BELIEVE.[7]

Happiness is the mental state of contentment which comes from *successful adaptation to the world as it really is*. It comes from being *useful*, of contributing to the welfare and happiness of others.[8]

Why destroy present happiness by a distant misery, which *may never come* at all?—for every substantial grief has twenty shadows, and most of the shadows *of your own making*.[9]

When a bit of sunshine hits ye After passing of a cloud, When a bit of laughter gets ye And ye're spine is feeling proud Don't forget to up and fling it At a soul that's feeling blue. For the minit that ye sling it, It's a *boomerang* for you.[10]

A laugh is just like music, It lingers in the heart, And where its melody is heard, The ills of life depart;[11]

You should realize that—
If you were busy being *kind*, Before you knew it, you would find You'd soon forget to think 'twas true That someone was unkind to you.

If you were busy being glad, And cheering people who are sad, Although your heart might ache a bit, You'd soon forget to notice it.[12]

The delights of thought, of truth, of work, and of well doing will not descend upon us like the dew upon the flower, without effort of our own. Labor, watchfulness, perseverance, self-denial, fortitude, are the elements out of which this kind of joy is formed.[13]

The happiness of a man in this life does not consist in the *absence* but in the MASTERY of his passions.[14]

Virtue alone is happiness below.[15]

Doing good is the only certainly happy action of a man's life.[16]

Happier?—That would mean more contented with my station in life, striving to derive all possible benefits from it, to BEAUTIFY rather than alter it.[17]

My friend, do you know why the work you accomplish fails either to give pleasure to yourself or others? It is because it is not *cheerfully* done, and therefore appears discolored.[18]

The world is so full of a number of things, I'm sure we should all be as happy as kings.[19]

And now I exhort you to be of good cheer.[20]

Live for something, *have a purpose*, And that purpose keep in view; Drifting like a helmless vessel, Thou cans't ne'er to life be true.[21]

My crown is *in my heart*, not on my head; Not deck'd with diamonds, and Indian stones, For to be seen; my crown is called *content*; A crown it is that seldom Kings enjoy.[22]

There are two ways of being happy; we may either diminish our wants or augment our means; either will do.[23]

For pleasures are like poppies spread: you seize the flower the bloom is shed.[24]

> Here's a motto, just your fit—
> Laugh a little bit.
> When you think you're trouble hit,
> Laugh a little bit.
> Look misfortune in the face,
> Brave the beldam's rude grimace;
> Ten to one 'twill yield its place,
> If you have the wit and grit
> Just to laugh a little bit.
>
> *Keep* your face with *sunshine* LIT.
> Laugh a little bit.[25]

If you should have the slightest difficulty in keeping a smile upon your face, just *keep your* HEART *smiling*. When his heart smiles, one is so filled with smiles and happiness that his countenance just breaks forth into smiling. The smiles of the smiling heart are not cold or assumed; consequently when the warm, generous smiles of the smiling heart express themselves, smiles radiate in every direction. In the smiling heart is Love and God.[26]

> *Laugh* and the *world laughs* with you,
> Weep and you weep ALONE.

Rejoice and men will seek you,
 Grieve, and they turn and go:
They want full measure of your pleasure,
 But they do not want your *woe*.[27]

Do not let your personal feelings of discouragement, fatigue, disgust, hate, or fear show in your facial expression nor allow them to make their impression on your personality. Their impressions CAN *be prevented, but you will have to be watchful.*

WORK IS ONE KEY TO HAPPINESS.[28]

To be constantly employed, and never asking "What shall I do?" is the secret of much goodness and happiness.[29]

There is a time in life when we bemoan the fact that light-hearted joyousness of youth has left us. We blame our circumstances, environment, and associates. Some go in search of that which is gone. Do not let such a loss disturb you. In due time that which you think is lost will emerge again in a bigger, deeper, joy—tranquility—the crown of patience, suffering, and faith.

Spirit (of joyousness), that rarely comest now, And only to contrast my gloom . . . thou once didst dwell With me year-long. A moment glimpsed, then seen no more,— Thou whose swift footsteps we can trace *Away* from every mortal door . . . 'Tis I am changed, not thou art fleet: The man thy presence feels again, Not in the blood, but in the brain, . . . Wayward, when once we feel thy lack, 'Tis worse than vain to woo thee back; Yet there is one who seems to be thine elder sister, She is not that for which youth hoped, But she hath blessings all her own, Almost I deem that it is thou (joyousness) Come back with graver matron brow, But "No," she answers, "I am she whom the Gods love, Tranquility; That other whom you seek forlorn, half earthly was; but I am born of the immortals, HE WINS ME LATE, BUT KEEPS ME LONG."[30]

THOUGHTS CAN ESTABLISH HAPPINESS

It is as essential to control our thoughts as it is to control our actions. We are careful that our actions are good, clean and gracious, and it is even more important that our thoughts be likewise for:

"AS A MAN THINKETH IN HIS HEART SO IS HE."[31]

The mind is its own place, and in itself Can make a *heaven of hell, a hell of heaven.*[32]

If instead of a gem, or even a flower, we could cast the *gift of a lovely thought* into the heart of a friend, that would be giving as the angels must give.[33]

No benefactor is equal to him who peoples life with new and lofty ideals.[34]

> For that thou *seest* man,
> That too *become* thou must,
> GOD, if thou *seest* God;
> Dust, if thou *SEEST* dust.[35]

THINKING GOOD IS THANKING GOD.[36]

Ideals are like stars: you will not succeed in touching them with your hands, but like the seafaring man on the ocean desert of waters, you choose them as your *guides*, and, *following* them, you *reach your destiny*.[37]

The thoughts which nestle within us, and issue from us in language and in act, determine our moral character. The most exquisite piece of sculpture which Michelangelo or Rodin ever carved, was ONCE only a THOUGHT.[38]

Men should be judged, not by their tint of skin, The Gods they serve, the vintage that they drink, Nor by the way they fight, love, or sin,
But *by the* QUALITY OF THOUGHTS THEY THINK.[39]

I will govern my *life,* and my *thought,* as if the whole world were to *see* the one, and to *read* the other.[40]

The thought that leads to no action is not thought—it is dreaming.[41]

The happiest people in the world are those who have the most interesting thoughts.[42]

We live in deeds, not years; in thoughts, not breaths; in feelings, not in figures on the dial; we should count time by heart throbs. He most lives who THINKS most, FEELS *the noblest,* ACTS *the best.*[43]

May we have high erected thoughts seated in the heart of courtesy.[44]

Do you know that your thoughts rule your life, Be they pure or impure in the strife? As you *think—so you are,* And you *make* or you *mar* Your success in the world By your *Thoughts.*[45]

Hitch your wagon to a star—but keep your feet on the ground.[46]

The pleasantest things in the world are pleasant thoughts and the great art in life is to have as many of them as possible.[47]

Then let your secret thoughts be fair—They have a *vital* part and share, In *shaping words* and *molding fate;* God's system is so intricate.[48]

You can never tell what your THOUGHTS will do In bringing you hate or love; For THOUGHTS ARE THINGS, and their airy wings Are swifter than carrier doves. They follow the *law of the universe,*—EACH THING MUST CREATE ITS KIND; And they speed o'er the track to *bring you back* Whatever went out from your mind.[49]

John Ruskin says, "I believe every *right* action and *true* thought sets the seal of its beauty on *person* and *face.*"

Why *imagine* evil intentions against yourself? Cannot you see how the thought troubles and disquiets you?[50]

Whene'er a noble deed is wrought, Whene'er is spoken a noble thought, Our hearts, in glad surprise, To higher levels rise.[51]

Whatsoever things are *true,* whatsoever things are *just,* whatsoever things are *pure,* whatsoever things are *lovely* —THINK ON THESE THINGS.[52]

There is nothing either good or bad, but *thinking* makes it so.[53]

As *thou hast* BELIEVED, so be it done unto thee.[54]

REFLECTIONS

*This truth of the importance of thoughts is not a modern
idea of any cult of religion or of modern psychology. It is
part of the foundation of life and was laid down for us along
with other truths in The Bible. For many centuries it has
been ignored, but the light of its truth is beginning to reach
dark places.*

*Thoughts shape one's fate, determining success or failure.
Each thought stamps itself forever on one's personality—
thoughts therefore, make one's personality.*

*There are so many beautiful things in the world—so much
goodness to learn that there is not room in the human heart
to hold all of the loveliness. Every time a destructive or ugly
thought enters the mind it crowds out a good thought. The
wise man learns to control his mind so that it will act con-
structively for his benefit. Sooner than we expect it pays
dividends. Tennyson says, "I am a part of all that I have
met."*

One of the most satisfying experiences in life is a deep appreciation of Nature. Wealth, health, friends and fame can be taken from us, but if we have a deep feeling for the beauty in Nature, we can still be happy.

At times, nature is so lovely that an individual feels thwarted because he is unable to express the emotions it arouses in his soul. Poems which accurately express these emotions help us to express ourselves.

"A thing of beauty is a joy forever. Its loveliness increases; it will never pass into nothingness."[1]

Nature always wears the color of the spirit.[2]

To me the meanest *flower* that blows *can give thoughts* that do often lie too deep for tears.[3]

Flowers in June give us memories for December:

I wandered lonely as a cloud That floats on high o'er vales and hills, When all at once I saw a crowd, A host, of golden daffodils; Beside the lake, beneath the trees, Fluttering and dancing in the breeze.   Continuous as the stars that shine And twinkle on the milky way, They stretched in never-ending line Along the margin of the bay; Ten thousand saw I at a glance Tossing their heads in sprightly dance.

The waves beside them danced; but they Out-did the
sparkling waves in glee; A poet could not be gay In such
a jocund company; I gazed—and gazed—but little thought
What wealth the show to me had brought;   For oft,
when on my couch I lie In vacant or in pensive mood,
They flash upon that inward eye Which is the bliss of
solitude, And then my heart with rapture thrills And dances
with the daffodils.[4]

*Be alert lest material interests callous our souls and prevent
us from identifying ourselves with nature:*

The world is too much with us; late and soon, Getting
and spending, WE LAY WASTE OUR POWERS; *Little we see in
nature that is ours;* We have given our hearts away, a sordid
boon—For *this,* for everything, WE ARE OUT OF TUNE.[5]

*Daytime has no exclusive right to the beauties of nature.
You will be the richer for taking this thought with you
into the night:*

Silently one by one in the infinite meadows of heaven,
Blossomed the lovely stars, the forget-me-nots of the angels.[6]

What is a flower?:

Flower in the crannied wall, I pluck you out of the cran-
nies, I hold you here, root and all, in my hand, Little flower
—but *if I could understand what you are, root and all,* and
all in all I should know what God and man is.[7]

In summer the soul of nature seems to expand:

And what is so rare as a day in June? Then, if ever, come
perfect days; Then heaven tries earth if it be in tune, And
over it softly her warm ear lay; Whether we *look,* or

whether we *listen, We hear life* murmur, *or see it* glisten;
Every *clod feels a stir of might, An instinct* within it *that
reaches and towers,* And, groping blindly above it for light,
Climbs to a soul in grass and flowers.

Now is the high-tide of the year, And *whatever of life
hath ebbed away Comes flooding back* with a ripply cheer,
In every bare inlet and creek and bay; Now the heart is
so full that a drop overfills it; We are happy now because
God wills it; No matter how barren the past may have been,
'Tis enough for us now that the leaves are green.

And the eyes *forget* the *tears they have shed,* The heart
forgets its sorrow and ache; The soul partakes the season's
youth, And the sulphurous rifts of passion and woe Lie deep
'neath a silence pure and smooth, Like burnt-out craters
healed with snow.[8]

Here is something to remember when the first snow falls:

The snow had begun in the gloaming, And busily all the
night Had been *heaping fields* and highway *With a silence
deep and white.*   *Every* pine and fir and hemlock Wore
ermine too dear for an earl, And the *poorest twig* on the elm
tree *Was ridged inch deep with pearl.*   From sheds new-
roofed with Carrara, Came Chanticleer's muffled crow, The
stiff rails were softened to swan's down, And still fluttered
down the snow.[9]

Winter brings a crisp, delicate beauty of its own:

Down swept the chill wind from the mountain peak,
From the snow five thousand summers old; On open wold
and hilltop bleak It had gathered all the cold, And whirled
it like sleet on the wanderer's cheek; It carried a shiver
everywhere From the unleafed boughs and pastures bare;
The little brook heard it and built a roof 'Neath which he
could house him, winter-proof.

All night by the white stars' frosty gleams He groined his arches and matched his beams Slender and clear were his *crystal spars* As the lashes of light that trim the stars; *He sculptured every summer delight In his halls and chambers* out of sight; Sometimes his tinkling waters slipt Down through a *frost-leaved forest crypt. Long, sparkling aisles of steel-stemmed trees* Bending to counterfeit a breeze; Sometimes the roof no fretwork knew But *silvery mosses that downward grew* Sometimes it was carved in sharp relief With *quaint arabesques of ice-fern leaf* Sometimes it was simply smooth and clear For the gladness of heaven to shine through . . . *No mortal builder's most rare device Could match this winter palace of ice.*[10]

When you enter a rich woodland—consider:

This is the forest primeval. The *murmuring pines* and the hemlocks, *Bearded with moss,* and in garments green, indistinct in the twilight, Stand like Druids of old, *with voices sad and prophetic; Stand like harpers hoar, with beards that rest on their bosoms.* Speaks, and in accents disconsolate answers the wail of the forest. This is the forest primeval; but where are the hearts that beneath it Leaped like the doe when he hears in the woodland the voice of the huntsman?[11]

The treasures of nature are open to all who will see them:

Then the little Hiawatha *Learned of every bird its language,* Learned their names and *all their secrets,* How they built their nests in summer, Where they hid themselves in winter, *Talked with them* whene'er he met them, Called them "Hiawatha's Chickens." *Of all the beasts he learned the language,* Learned their names and *all their secrets,* How the beavers built their lodges, Where the squirrels hid their acorns, How the reindeer ran so swiftly, Why the rabbit was so timid, *Talked with them* whene'er he met them, Called them "*Hiawatha's* BROTHERS."[12]

When depressed or sorrowful:

My garden spade can heal; a woodland walk, a quest of river grapes, a mocking thrush a wild rose, a rock loving columbine, salve my worst wounds.[13]

Do you realize all that music can do for your spirit?

Seated one day at the organ, I was weary and ill at ease, And my fingers wandered idly Over the noisy keys. I do not know what I was playing Or what I was dreaming then; But I struck one chord of music Like the sound of a *great Amen.*

It flooded the crimson twilight Like the close of an angel's psalm, And it *lay on my fevered spirit With a touch of infinite calm.* It *quieted* pain and sorrow, *Like love overcoming strife,* It seemed the *harmonious echo From our discordant life.* It *linked all perplexed meanings Into one perfect peace.* And trembled away into silence, As if it were loath to cease.

I have sought, but I seek it vainly, That *one lost chord divine,* That *came from the soul of the organ* And *entered into mine. It may be that Death's bright angel Will speak in that chord again,* It may be that only in heaven I shall hear that grand Amen.[14]

THE HEAVENS DECLARE THE GLORY OF GOD; AND THE FIRMAMENT SHEWETH HIS HANDIWORK.[15]

And this, our life, exempt from public haunt Finds tongues in trees, books in running brooks, Sermons in stones, and *good in everything.*[16]

Clear, placid Leman. Thy contrasted lake, With the wild world I dwelt in, is a thing Which warns me, with its stillness, to forsake Earth's troubled waters for a purer spring.[17]

And just in case conceit forms a stumbling stone preventing you from travelling the road to happiness, remember—

MAN'S LITTLENESS IN PRESENCE OF THE STARS

Thou, proud man, look upon yon starry vault, Survey the countless gems which richly stud The night's imperial chariot;—Telescopes Will show the *myriads more*, innumerous As the sea-sand;—each of those little lamps Is the great source of light, the central sun Round which some other mighty sisterhood Of planets travel,—every planet stocked With living beings important as thee. Now, proud man,—now, where is thy greatness fled? What art thou in the scale of universe? Less, less than nothing![18]

Let yourself respond to nature. It will enrich you spiritually.

To-day I have *grown taller* from walking with the trees,
The seven-sister-poplars who go softly in line;
And I think my *heart is whiter* for its parley with a star
That trembled out at nightfall and hung above a pine.[19]

There is balm in the open fields:

The little cares that fretted me, I lost them yesterday
Among the fields above the sea, Among the winds at play;
Among the lowing of the herds, The rustling of the trees,
Among the singing of the birds, The humming of the bees.
The foolish fears of what may happen, I cast them all away Among the clover-scented grass, Among the new-mown hay; Among the husking of the corn Where drowsy poppies nod, Where *ill thoughts die and good are born, Out in the fields with God.*[20]

And religion in gardens:

> A garden is a lovesome thing, God wot;
>   Rose plot,
> Fringed pool,
>   Ferned grot,
> The veriest school of peace:
> And yet the *fool*
>   Contends that God is *not*.
> Not God, in gardens! When the eve is cool!
>   Nay, but I have a sign,
> 'TIS VERY SURE GOD WALKS IN MINE![21]

The calm faith of homing waterfowl holds a lesson for everyone:

Whither, 'midst falling dew, While glow the heavens with the last steps of day, Far, through their rosy depths, dost thou pursue Thy solitary way?   *There is a Power whose care Teaches thy way along that pathless coast*—The desert and illimitable air—Lone wandering, but not lost.
Thou'rt gone! The abyss of heaven Hath swallowed up thy form; yet on my heart *Deeply hath sunk the lesson thou hast given,* And shall not soon depart.   *He* who, from zone to zone, Guides through the boundless sky thy certain flight, In the *long way that I must tread* ALONE *Will lead my steps aright.*[22]

Learn the warm companionship of nature:

Across the lonely beach we flit, One little sandpiper and I, And fast I gather, bit by bit, The scattered driftwood, bleached and dry. The wild waves reach their hands for it. The wild wind raves, the tide runs high, As up and down the beach we flit, One little sandpiper and I.

I watch him as he skims along, Uttering his sweet and mournful cry; He starts not at my fitful song, Nor flash of fluttering drapery He has no thought of any wrong He scans me with a fearless eye; Stanch friends are we, well tried and strong The little sandpiper and I.

Comrade, where wilt thou be to-night, When the loosed storm breaks furiously? My driftwood fire will burn so bright. To what warm shelter canst thou fly? *I do not fear for thee, though wroth* The tempest rushes through the sky; For *are we not God's Children both, Thou, little sandpiper, and I?*[23]

The glorious skylark—however high its flight—returns, contented to its home:

Ethereal minstrel, pilgrim of the sky,
Dost thou despise the earth where cares abound?
Or, while the wings aspire, are heart and eye
Both with thy nest upon the dewy ground?
Thy nest which thou canst drop into at will,
Those quivering wings composed, that music still.

Leave to the nightingale her shady wood;
A privacy of glorious light is thine;
Whence thou dost pour upon the world a flood
Of harmony, with instinct more divine;
Type of the wise who soar, but never roam;
True to the kindred points of Heaven and Home![24]

The groves were God's first temples. Ere man learned
To hew the shaft and lay the architrave,
And spread the roof above them,—ere he framed
The lofty vault, to gather and roll back

The sound of anthems; in the darking wood
Amidst the cool and silence, he knelt down
And offered to the Mightiest, solemn thanks
And supplication.[25]

Be aware of life around you:

Walk with thy fellow-creatures; note the hush and whispers
among them. There is not a sprig or leaf but hath his morning hymn; each bush and oak doth know *I am.* Canst *thou*
not *sing?*[26]

The hills have a message for those who understand:

I need not shout my faith. Thrice eloquent Are quiet trees
and the green listening sod; Hushed are the stars, whose
power is never spent. The *hills are mute; yet how they speak
of God!*[27]

Within a garden one may find himself:

The kiss of the sun for pardon, The song of the birds for
mirth,—*One is nearer God's heart in a garden Than any-
where else on earth.*[28]

The rainbow is a symbol of hope:

My *heart leaps up* when I behold A *rainbow* in the sky;
So was it when my life began; So is it now I am a man;
So be it when I shall grow old, Or let me die![29]

Nature has so much to teach us:

Up! up! my friend, and quit your book; Or surely you'll
grow double; Up! up! my friend and clear your looks; Why
all this toil and trouble?   The sun, above the mountain
head, A freshening lustre mellow Through all the long green

fields has spread, His first sweet evening yellow.   Books! 'tis a dull and endless strife; Come, hear the woodland linnet, How sweet his music, on my life There's more of wisdom in it.   And hark, how blithe the throstle sings! He, too, is no mean preacher; Come forth into the light of things, *Let Nature be your teacher.*

She has a world of ready wealth, Our minds and hearts to bless—Spontaneous wisdom breathed by health, Truth breathed by cheerfulness.   One impulse from a vernal wood May teach you more of man, Of moral evil and of good, Than all the sages can.   Sweet is the lore which Nature brings; Our meddling intellect Misshapes the beauteous forms of things;—We murder to dissect.   Enough of Sciences and of Art; Close up those barren leaves; Come forth, and *bring with you a heart that* WATCHES *and* RECEIVES.[30]

The sun, the moon, the stars, the seas, the hills and the plains—Are not *these, O Soul, the vision of Him* who reigns? Is not the vision He? tho' he be not that which He seems? Dreams are true while they last, and do we not live in dreams?   Earth, these solid stars, this weight of body and limb, Are they not sign and symbol of thy division from Him? *Dark is the world to thee? Thyself are the reason why:* For is He not all but thou, who has power to feel "I am I?"[31]

REFLECTION

To be richly and completely content one must be in harmony with the universe and its laws—trained to appreciate all laws and all nature. When we are confused, our greatest comfort is to commune with nature away from the haunts of men. Most of us have eyes and ears but we see little in nature that is ours. For nature, for everything we are out of tune.

We can learn to know the language of the flowers and hear the morning hymn of the grasses, so that we can closely identify ourselves with the murmur and gleam of life and thrill with birds in the sun. Let our love of nature stir the soul with beauty. Association with nature helps keep that emotional balance which we need so greatly in our frantic struggle of life. All hurts, the worst of human wounds/those of the spirit/can be healed in a garden.

In nature's haunts we can fill our hearts so full of loveliness that there is no room for ugly thoughts. Let us put ourselves in touch with the great laws of the spirit, that we may link the chain of brotherhood.

When we stand on the shores of an ocean and gaze across the boundless deep, up into the vast unknown, into the spaceless universe, we realize how small all petty, earth-bound differences are.

"He who serves his brother best, gets nearer God than all the rest." When we realise this great, basic truth we can see and understand that each of us, as "parts of one tremendous whole" has a purpose. Each individual, each nation has a contribution to make and should make it to the perfection of the whole.

The musician gives his interpretation of Deity—of Truth —Perfection—in music; the gardener plants seeds and helps them "climb to a soul in grass and flowers;" the artist interprets through color; the poet weaves his version with words; the physician relieves suffering. All praise God in their own way; the bird trilling its joy; the flower giving its perfume. The measure is not what we do, nor how much we do but— how well we do it: "Each in his separate star shall paint the thing as he sees it, for the God of things as they are."

If one organ of the body fails to play its part the whole

body reacts trying to compensate for the erring one. If insects, persons or animals in life fail in their part, all humanity suffers—for all are one. The same law holds for nations as for individuals.

The great symphony "Life" composed of many parts is played in many moods with occasional solos on the one theme, played by many individuals in unison, though some may be out of tune, 'tis true—

Let us train ourselves to see and know this "oneness" in the plan of our Maker, so that we may realize the need of appreciation of understanding, of kindliness, to bring about harmony in life's Great Symphony, and thus help to bring about the great Hallelujah Chorus, "Peace on Earth, Good Will to Men!"

3 HERE IS ENCOURAGEMENT

Encouragement may be found here to meet every kind of trial and discouragement with fortitude. For some, this chapter may be a magic key to unlock the door to ultimate achievement despite seemingly unsurmountable obstacles.

"Meet every adverse circumstance as its master. Don't let it master you."

"Defeat may serve as well as victory to shake the soul and let the glory out."[1]

There is always the battle to be fought before the victory is won.[2] Too many think they must have the victory *before the Battle.*

Our greatest glory is not in never falling, but in rising every time we fall.[3]

If what shows afar so grand, Turn to nothing in thy hand, On again; the VIRTUE lies in the STRUGGLE, not the prize.[4]

> Build for yourself a strong-box,
>   Fashion each part with care;
> When it's strong as your hand can make it,
>   Put all your troubles there;

Hide there all thought of your failures
  And each bitter cup that you quaff;
Lock all your heartaches within it,
  Then sit on the lid and *laugh.*

Tell no one else its contents,
  Never its secrets share;
When you've dropped in your care and your worry
  Keep them forever there;
Hide them from sight so completely
  That the world will never dream half;
Fasten the strong-box securely—
  Then sit on the lid and laugh.[5]

Fear not, for *that which thou fearest shall come upon thee.*[6]

And *Patience* wins the race.

Never despair, but if you do, work on in despair.

When the weather suits you not,
  Try smiling;
When your coffee isn't hot,
  Try smiling.
When your neighbors don't do right,
Or your relatives all fight,
Sure 'tis hard but then you might—
  Try smiling.

Doesn't change the things, of course—
  Just smiling;
But *it cannot make them worse,*
  Just smiling.

And it seems to help your case,
Brightens up a gloomy place;
Then, it sort o' rests your face—
    Just smiling.[7]

Great minds have purposes, others have wishes. Little minds are tamed and subdued by misfortune; but great minds rise above it.[8]

BE NOT IMPATIENT. Think of God's great patience in his work with man through the ages to bring about "Peace on Earth" and Heaven here.[9]

Then, *welcome* each rebuff that turns earth's smoothness rough, *each sting* that *bids not sit nor stand, but go.*[10]

    When we sigh about our trouble
      It grows double
        Every day;
    When we laugh about our trouble
      It's a bubble
        Blown away.[11]

He giveth more grace when the burdens grow greater, He sendeth *more strength* when the labors increase; To added affliction He addeth his mercy, To multiplied trials, *His* multiplied *peace.*   When we have *exhausted* our store of *endurance,* When our strength has failed ere the day is half done, When we reach the end of our hoarded resources, *Our Father's* full *giving is only begun.*

His love has no limit, His grace has no measure, His power no boundary known unto men; For out of his infinite riches in Jesus He giveth and giveth and giveth again.[12]

Whenever you feel that you as an individual can do little, remember:

The course of history shows that many a time a STRONG, EARNEST *soul has swayed the destiny of nations.*

And let us not be weary in well-doing; for in due season we shall reap, if we faint not.[13]

Firm must be the will, *patient* the heart, *passionate* the aspiration, to secure the fulfilment of *some high and lonely purpose,* when reverie spreads always its bed of roses on the one side, and practical work summons to its treadmill on the other.[14]

In all lives *there is a crisis* in the formation of character. It comes from many causes, and from some which, on the surface, are apparently trivial. But the result is the same— *a sudden revelation to our selves of our secret purpose* and a recognition of our, perhaps long shadowed but now masterful, convictions.[15]

WHEN ONCE THOU HAST CONCEIVED AND DETERMINED THY MISSION WITHIN THY SOUL, LET NAUGHT ARREST THY STEPS.[16]

If the power to do hard work is not talent, it is the best possible substitute for it.[17]

Success is not a matter of luck or of genius. Success depends on *adequate preparation* and indomitable determination.

Your Father knoweth what things ye have need of *before* ye ask him.[18]

It is the *last step* in a race that *counts;* It is the *last stroke* on the nail that counts; *Many a prize has been lost* JUST WHEN IT WAS READY TO BE PLUCKED.[19]

It is the difference in viewpoint which makes success or defeat in "Opportunity:"

Thus I beheld, or dreamed it in a dream:—There spread a cloud of dust along a plain; And underneath the cloud, or in it, raged A furious battle, and men yelled, and swords Shocked upon swords and shields. A prince's banner Wavered, then staggered backward, hemmed by foes.

A craven hung along the battle's edge, *And thought,* "Had I a sword of keener steel*—That blue blade that the king's son bears—but *this* Blunt thing—!" He snapt and flung it from his hand,* And lowering crept away and left the field. Then came the *king's son,* wounded, sore beset, And *weaponless,* and *saw the broken sword,* Hilt-buried in the dry and trodden sand, And ran and *snatched it,* and with a battle shout Lifted afresh, he *hewed his enemy down,* And saved a great cause that heroic day.[20]

Many men owe the GRANDEUR of their lives to their TRE-MENDOUS *difficulties.*[21]

ADVERSITY is the *prosperity* of the great. Kites rise AGAINST, not *with,* the wind.[22]

> If you *think* you are *beaten,* you *are;*
> If you *think* you dare not, you don't.
> If you'd like to win, but think you can't,
> It's almost a cinch you won't.
> If you think you'll lose, you're lost,
> For out in the world we find

Success *begins* with a fellow's *will*;
It's *all in the state of mind.*

Life's battles don't always go
To the stronger or faster man;
But soon or late the man who wins
Is the one who *thinks* he can.[23]

FAITH NEVER FAILS: It is a miracle worker. It looks beyond all boundaries, transcends all limitations, penetrates all obstacles and sees the goal.[24]

If impatient with daily tasks it should help to realize that:

Drudgery is as *necessary* to call out the treasures of the *mind* as harrowing and planting those of the earth.[25]

And Jesus saith, "Have faith in God. For verily I say unto you, that whosoever shall say unto this mountain, Be thou removed, and be thou cast into the sea; and shall not doubt in his heart, but shall believe that those things he saith shall come to pass; he shall have whatsoever he saith.

"Therefore I say unto you, whatsoever things ye desire when ye pray, *believe that ye receive them,* and ye shall have them."[26]

To suffer woes which Hope thinks infinite; To forgive wrongs darker than death or night; To defy power, which seems omnipotent; To love, and bear; to hope till HOPE CREATES FROM ITS OWN WRECK THE THING IT CONTEMPLATES; Neither to change, nor falter, nor repent; This is, like thy glory, Titan, to be Good, great and joyous, beautiful and free; This is alone Life, Joy, Empire, and Victory.[27]

Full many a gem of purest ray serene The dark unfathomed caves of ocean bear Full many a flower, is born to blush unseen; And waste its sweetness on the desert air.[28]

When you get into a tight place and everything goes against you, till it seems as though you COULD NOT HOLD ON A MINUTE LONGER, NEVER GIVE UP THEN, for THAT is JUST the place and time that THE TIDE WILL TURN.[29]

This is one of the greatest truths. It is encouraging to know that greater souls than ours come to those places which they can neither go over, around, or through. But by holding on —a little past the human endurance point the difficulty is overcome and disappears.

He who loses wealth loses *much*; He who loses a friend loses *more*: But he that loses his courage *loses all*.[30]

God answers prayer; sometimes, when hearts are weak,
He gives the very gifts believers seek.
But often faith must learn a deeper test,
And *TRUST GOD'S SILENCE WHEN HE DOES
    NOT SPEAK;*
For He whose name is Love will send the best.
Stars may burn out, nor mountain walls endure,
But God is true, *HIS PROMISES ARE SURE*
    For those who seek.[31]

DON'T WEAR YOUR WISH-BONE WHERE YOUR BACK-BONE OUGHT TO BE![32]

Count that day lost whose low descending sun
Views from thy hand no worthy action done.[33]

He came up smiling—used to say
He made his fortune that-a-way;
He had hard luck a-plenty, too,
But settled down and fought her through;
An' every time he *got a jolt*
He just *took on a tighter holt*,
Slipped back some when he tried to climb
But came up smilin' every time.

He came up smilin'—good for him!
He had th' grit an' pluck an' vim,
So he's on Easy Street, an' durned
If I don't think his luck is earned!
No matter if he lost sometimes,
He's *got th' stuff in him that climbs*,
An' when his chance was mighty-slim,
He came up smilin'—good fer him![34]

Thrice blessed is he who, when all is drear and cheerless within and without, when his teachers terrify him, and his friends shrink from him, obstinately clings to moral good.[35]

"FEAR NOT, I am with thee; Oh, be not dismayed,
For *I am thy God*, and will still give thee aid."[36]

Of all the work that produces results, *nine-tenths must be drudgery*. There is *no work*, from the highest to the lowest, which *can be done well by any man* who is *unwilling to make that sacrifice*. Part of the very nobility of the devotion of the true workman to his work consists in the fact that a man is not daunted by finding that drudgery must be done . . . And there is nothing which so truly repays itself as this very perseverance against weariness.[37]

Oh, for the faith and strength to win
Every battle we begin.
Oh, for patience to put through
Every task we plan to do.[38]

Defeat may serve as well as victory to shake the soul and
let the glory out.

. . . .

Only the soul that knows the mighty grief can know the
mighty rapture. Sorrows come To stretch out spaces in the
heart for joy.[39]

When the battle breaks against you and the crowd forgets
    to cheer
When the anvil chorus echoes with the essence of a *jeer;*
When the knockers start their panning in the knocker's
    nimble way
With a rap for all your errors and a josh upon your play—
There is *one quick answer ready* that will nail them on the
    wing;
There is one reply forthcoming that will wipe away the
    sting;
There is one elastic come-back that will hold them as it
    should—
Make good!

No matter where you finish in the mix-up or the row.
There are those among the rabble who *will pan you anyhow;*
But the entry who is sticking and delivering the stuff
Can listen to the yapping as he giggles up his cuff;
The loafer has no come-back and the quitter no reply
When the Anvil Chorus echoes, as it will, against the sky;
But there's one quick answer ready that will wrap them in
    a hood—
Make good![40]

Men at some times are masters of their fates;
The fault is not in our stars,
But *in ourselves,* that we are underlings.[41]

To THINK A THING IS IMPOSSIBLE IS TO MAKE IT SO. Courage is victory, timidity's defeat.[42]

All the performances of human art, at which we look with praise and wonder, are instances of the resistless force of perseverance.[43]

The world is waiting for somebody, Waiting and watching today; Somebody to lift and strengthen, Somebody to shield and stay. Do you thoughtfully question, "Who?" 'Tis you, my friend, *'tis you.*

The world is waiting for somebody, The sad world, black and cold, When wan-faced *children are watching For hope in the eyes of the old.* Do you wondering question, *"Who?"* 'Tis you, my friend, *'tis you!*

The world is waiting for somebody, And has been years on years; Somebody to *soften its sorrows,* Somebody to heed its tears, Then, doubting, question no longer, "Who?" For, oh, my friend, *'tis you.*[44]

My name's DEFEAT—but through the bitter fight,
　　To those who know, I'M SOMETHING MORE THAN
　　　　FRIEND;
For I can build beyond the wrath of might
　　And drive away all yellow from the blend;
For those who quit, I am the final blow,
　　But for the brave who seek their chance to learn,
I show the way, at last, beyond the foe,
　　To where the scarlet flames of triumph burn.[45]

Never give up! it is wiser and better
  Always to hope, than ever despair;
Fling off the load of Doubt's cankering fetter,
  And break the dark spell of tyrannical Care.
NEVER GIVE UP! Or the burdens may sink you;
  Providence kindly has mingled the cup,
And in all trials and troubles, bethink you,
  The watchword of life must be, "NEVER *give up!*"[46]

All things are possible to him that believeth.[47]

If God be for us, *who* can be against us?[48]

Don't be foolish and get sour when things don't come your
    way—
Don't be a pampered baby and declare, "Now I won't play."
  Just go on grinning and bear it;
  Have you heartache? Millions share it,
  If you EARN a crown, you'll wear it—
     Keep sweet.

Don't go handing out your troubles to your busy fellow-
    men—
If you whine around they'll try to keep from meeting you
    again;
  Don't declare the world's "agin" you,
  Don't let pessimism win you,
  Prove there's lots of good stuff in you—
     KEEP SWEET.[49]

  Life is a game with a glorious prize,
    If we can only play it right.
  It is give and take, build and break,
    And often it ends in a fight;

But he surely wins who honestly tries
    Regardless of wealth or fame,
He can never despair who plays it fair—
    How are YOU playing the game?

Do you wilt and whine, if you fail to win
    In the manner you think your due?
Do you sneer at the man in case that he can
    And does, do better than you?
Do you take your rebuffs with a knowing grin?
    Do you laugh tho' you pull up lame?
Does your faith hold true when the whole world's
        blue?
    How are YOU playing the game?[50]

Great achievement often requires long, tortuous, bitter experiences. One has to resist ruthless persecution physically and mentally; win complete mastery of himself. One must rise above disappointments, neglect and sorrow. Through loneliness of spirit one learns to understand the wisdom of the Universe.

Often you may have to make a bitter choice. Then, when you do ALL *in your power the Divine force will help you to your goal.*

How stimulating it is to realize that:

When nature wants to drill a man
And thrill a man,
And skill a man,
When Nature wants to mold a man
To play the noblest part
When she yearns with all her heart
To create so great and bold a man
That all the world shall praise—

Watch her method, watch her ways!
How she *ruthlessly perfects*
Whom she royally elects;
How she *hammers him* and hurts him
And with *mighty blows converts* him
Into trial shapes of clay which only
      Nature understands—
While his tortured heart is crying and
      he lifts beseeching hands—
How *she bends*, but never breaks,
When his good she undertakes . . .
How she uses whom she chooses
And with every purpose fuses him,
By every art induces him
To try his splendor out—
Nature knows what she's about.

When Nature wants to take a man
And shake a man
And wake a man;
When Nature wants to make a man
To do the future's will;
When she tries with all her skill
And she yearns with all her soul
To create him large and whole . . .
With what cunning she prepares him!
How she goads and *never spares him,*
How she whets him and she frets him
And in poverty begets him . . .
How *she often disappoints*
Whom she sacredly anoints,
With what wisdom she will hide him,
Never minding what betide him

Though his genius sob with slighting and
          his pride may not forget.
Bids him struggle harder yet.
Makes him lonely
So that only
God's high messages shall reach him
So that *she may surely teach* him
What the Hierarchy planned.
Though he may not understand
Gives him passions to command—
How remorselessly she spurs him,
With terrific ardor stirs him
When she poignantly prefers him!

When Nature wants to name a man
And fame a man
And tame a man
When Nature wants to shame a man
To do his heavenly best . . .
When she tries the highest test
That her reckoning may bring—
When she reins him and restrains him
So his body scarce contains him
While she fires him
And inspires him.
Keeps him yearning, ever burning for
          a tantalizing goal—
Lures and lacerates his soul,
Sets a challenge for his spirit,
Draws it higher when he's near it—
Makes a jungle, that he clear it;
Makes a desert, that he fear it
And subdue it if he can—
So doth Nature make a man.

Then to test his spirit's wrath
Hurls a mountain in his path—
Puts a bitter choice before him.
"Climb, or perish," so she says . . .
Watch her purpose, watch her ways!

Nature's plan is wondrous kind
Could we understand her mind . . .
Fools are they who call her blind.
When his feet are torn and bleeding
Yet his higher powers speeding
Blazing newer paths and fine;
When the force that is divine
Leaps to challenge every failure and his
    ardor still is sweet
And *love and hope are burning in the*
    presence of defeat . . .
Lo, the crisis! Lo, the shout
That must call the leader out!
When the people need salvation
Doth he come to lead the nation . . .
Thus doth Nature show her plan
When the world has found—a man![51]

Sure there is lots of trouble, Sure there are heaps of cares,
Burdens that bend us double, Worries that come to wear.
But we must keep pursuing Something, and see it through;
Still to be up and doing Is all that there is to do.

Though you would like to idle, Wait for the world to
right, Keep your hand on the bridle, Fight when you have
to fight. Women are won by wooing, Fortune is won the
same, And to be up and doing Is all there is to the game.

Few ever fail by trying, *Few ever win who wait.* All of
your *sitting, sighing Never will conquer fate.* Whatever path

you're hewing, One thing is certain, son; Either be up and
doing Or soon you'll be down and done.[52]

Enamored architect of airy rhyme
Build as thou wilt; *heed not what each man says;*
Good souls, but innocent of dreamer's ways,
Will come, and marvel why thou wastest time;
Others, beholding how thy turrets climb
'Twixt theirs and heaven, *will hate thee all thy days;*
But most beware of those who come to praise.
O Wondersmith, O worker in sublime
And heaven-sent dreams, let art be all in all;
Build as thou wilt, unspoiled by praise or blame,
Build as thou wilt, and as thy light is given:
Then, if at last the airy structure fall,
Dissolve, and vanish—take thyself no shame.
They fail, and they alone, who have not striven.[53]

I will lift up mine eyes unto the hills,
From whence cometh my help.
My help cometh from the Lord, which made
     heaven and earth.
He will not suffer thy foot to be moved:
He that keepeth thee will not slumber.
Behold, he that keepth Israel shall neither slum-
     ber nor sleep.
The Lord is thy keeper:
The Lord is thy shade upon thy right hand.
The Sun shall not smite thee by day, nor the
     moon by night,
The Lord shall preserve thee from all evil:
He shall preserve thy soul.[54]

GREAT THINGS ARE DONE WHEN MEN AND MOUNTAINS MEET;
THESE ARE NOT DONE BY JOSTLING IN THE STREET.[55]

There are times in one's life when all the world seems to
turn against us. Our motives are misunderstood, our words
misconstrued, a malicious smile or an unkind word reveals
to us the unfriendly feelings of others. Our advances are re-
pulsed, or met with icy coldness; a dry refusal arrests on our
lips the offer of help . . .

It is rare when injustice, or slights, patiently borne, do not
leave the heart at the close of day filled with a marvelous joy
and peace.

It is the seed God has sown, springing up and bearing
fruit.[56]

> Out of the night that covers me,
> Black as the pit from pole to pole,
> I thank whatever Gods may be
> For my *unconquerable soul.*
>
> It matters not how strait the gate,
> How charged with punishments the scroll,
> I am the *master* of my fate;
> I am the *captain* of my soul.[57]

Don't think when you have troubles that your *neighbor*
goes scot-free because he shows a smiling front And battles
cheerfully. No, man! He, too, has troubles, but herein the
difference lies, while you go idly moping round, The other
fellow *tries.*

Don't envy other people; maybe, if the truth you knew,
*you'd find their burdens heavier far than is the case with
you.* Because a fellow, rain or shine, Can show a smiling
face, Don't think you'd have an easier time If you could take
his place.[58]

Be strong and of good courage, fear not nor be afraid of them; for the Lord thy God, He it is that doth go with thee, He will not fail thee, nor forsake thee.[59]

GENIUS, that power which dazzles mortal eyes,
Is OFT BUT PERSEVERANCE IN DISGUISE.
  Continuous effort of itself implies,
  In spite of countless falls, the *power to rise*.
'Twixt failure and success the print's so fine,
Men sometimes know not when they touch the line;
Just when the pearl is waiting one more plunge,
How many a struggler has thrown up the sponge.
  As the tide goes clear out it comes clear in;
  In business 'tis at turns, the wisest win;
  And, oh, how true when shades of doubt dismay,
" 'TIS OFTEN DARKEST JUST BEFORE THE DAY."
  A little more persistence, courage, vim,
  Success will dawn o'er failure's cloudy rim.
  Then take this honey for the bitterest cup;
THERE IS NO FAILURE, SAVE IN GIVING UP.
  No real fall, so long as one still tries,
  For seeming set-backs make the strong man wise.
THERE'S NO DEFEAT, in truth, SAVE FROM WITHIN;
Unless you're beaten THERE, *you're bound to win*.[60]

This, then, is the main idea I hold—Existence, where it can, holds each at bay; It may be heat or hunger, pain or cold, But *there is always something* in the way *That each must batter down* to reach the goal Which does not lead to any flare or flame, But say—a *certain hardiness* of soul That does not fear the rigor of the game.[61]

It was a noble Roman, in Rome's imperial day, Who heard a coward croaker, before the Castle, say:

"They're safe in such a fortress; there is no way to shake it."

"On—On." exclaimed the hero, "I'll find a way, or make it."

Is Fame *your* aspiration? *Her path is steep and high;* in vain he seeks her temple, content to gaze and sigh; the shining throne is waiting, but he alone can take it who says, with Roman firmness, "I'LL FIND A WAY, OR MAKE IT."

Is Learning *your* ambition? *There is no royal road;* alike the peer and peasant must climb to her abode: Who feels the thirst of knowledge, In Helicon may slake it, If he has still the Roman will "I'LL FIND A WAY, OR MAKE IT."

Are Riches worth the getting? *They must be bravely sought;* with wishing and with fretting the boon cannot be bought; to all the prize is open, but only he can take it who says, with Roman courage, "I'LL FIND A WAY, OR MAKE IT."

In Love's impassioned warfare the tale has ever been, that victory crowns the valiant.—The brave are they who win: Though strong is Beauty's castle, a lover still may take it, who says, with Roman courage, "I'll FIND a way, or make it."[62]

I would be true, for there are those who trust me;
I would be pure, for there are those who care;
I would be strong, for there is much to suffer;
I would be brave, for there is much to dare.
I would be friend of all—the poor—the friendless;
I would be giving and forget the gift;
I would be humble, for I know my weakness;
I would look up—and laugh—and love—*and lift.*[63]

Discouraged? Remember:

When Abraham Lincoln was a young man he ran for the Legislature in Illinois and was badly swamped.

He next entered business, failed and spent seventeen years of his life paying up the debts of a worthless partner.

He was in love with a beautiful young woman to whom he became engaged—and then she died.

Later he married a woman who was a constant burden to him.

Entering politics again, he was badly defeated for Congress.

He failed to get an appointment to the U. S. Land Office.

He was badly defeated for the U. S. Senate.

In 1856 he became a candidate for the Vice Presidency and was again defeated.

In 1858 he was defeated by Douglas.

One failure after another—bad failures—great set-backs. In the face of all this he eventually became one of the country's greatest men, if not the greatest. When you think of a series of set-backs like this, doesn't it make you feel small to become discouraged, just because you think that you're having a hard time in life?[64]

The great were once as you.
They whom men magnify to-day
Once groped and blundered on life's way.
Were fearful of themselves, and thought
By *magic* was men's greatness wrought.
They feared to try what they could do;
Yet Fame hath crowned with her success
The *selfsame gifts that you possess.*

The great were young as you,
Dreaming the very dreams you hold,
Longing, yet fearing, to be bold,
Doubting that they *themselves* possessed
The strength and skill for every test,

Uncertain of the truths they knew,
Not sure that they could stand to fate
With all the courage of the great.

Then came a day when they
Their first bold venture made,
Scorning to cry for aid.
They dared to stand to fight alone,
Took up the gauntlet life had thrown,
Charged full-front to the gray,
Mastered their FEAR of self, and then
Learned that our *great men are but men.*

Oh, Youth, go forth and do!
You, too, to fame may rise;
You can be strong and wise.
Stand up to life and play the man—
You can if you'll but think you can;
The GREAT WERE ONCE AS YOU.
You envy them their proud success?
'TWAS WON WITH GIFTS THAT YOU POSSESS.[65]

Let us laugh, then, you and I,
Laugh, and see our troubles fly.
Fear, and *worry, sadness, doubt—*
These are things to *laugh* about.
We had lost them on the way
Had we but laughed yesterday.

Let us laugh, then; tuned to glee
What a life our life shall be;
Laughter, bubbling from within,
Is the heart's own medicine—
Life is better far by half
When we have but learned to laugh.[66]

If you have grave doubts that dismay you and bear you down, if you think that there is no chance for you—stop!

Each year sees new records set in almost every field. Better songs can be written, better radios can be made, more beautiful paintings can be painted.

Someone is going to do these things. Why should not YOU be the one to do some of them? But you must rise above present discouragement and keep driving steadily and cheerfully forward, as all great persons have had to do.

However the battle is ended,
   Though proudly the victor comes
With fluttering flags and prancing nags
   And echoing roll of drums,
Still truth proclaims this motto,
   In letters of living light—
No question is ever settled,
   Until it is settled right.

.   .   .   .

Let those who have failed take courage;
   Tho' the enemy seems to have won,
Tho' his ranks are strong, if he be in the wrong
   The battle is not yet done;
For, as sure as the morning follows
   The darkest hour of the night,
No question is ever settled
   Until it is settled right.

O man bowed down with labor;
   A woman, young, yet old;
O heart oppressed in the toiler's breast
   And crushed by the power of gold;
Keep on with your weary battle
   Against triumphant might;

No question is ever settled
Until it is settled right.[67]

Don't join the "I Could Have Club".

I am a charter member of the saddest club in town; we
hold meetin's on the corners, and we always wear a frown.

There's more'n a million members, and here, boys, is
the rub, *we've paid our dues forever* in the big "I Could
Have" Club.

Sam Brown says, "See that building? Well back in '23,
I could have bought the ground it's on for just a song,
ah me;"

John Smith answered sadly, "I could have bought on
Vine The Dyas place and play house The whole show for
a dime." . . . "I could have" is the pass word, "I wish I
had," the price; "I might have had," the memory; *"Ah, had
I had" how nice.*[68]

Men change, flags change, and border lines
    Move north or south, and east and west;
But still the great unaltered pines
    In centuries of green are dressed;
In warmer lands the quiet palm
    Still wears its calm;
TRUTH STANDS, GOD REIGNS, CHRIST WALKS TODAY.

. . . .

*The great unalterable things
    Will never change.* Though for a time
To other lands the bird takes wings,
    Though summer seeks some other clime,
Though for a time injustice hides
    The mountain sides—

Doubt not, fear not; work on, and wait;
   As sure as dawn shall conquer dark
So love will triumph over hate,
   And spring will bring again the lark.
Yes, if for truth you labor here,
   You need not fear.[69]

You should realize "The Test of Life!"

   What is a failure? It's only a spur
     To a man who receives it right,
   And it makes the spirit within him stir
     To go in once more and fight.
   If you never have *failed*, it's an easy guess
     You never have known a high success.

   What is a miss? It's a practice shot
     Which we often must make to enter
   The list of those who can hit the spot
     Of the bull's-eye in the center.
   If you never have sent your bullet wide,
     You never have put a mark inside.[70]

   We have to tread the mountain's base
     Before we reach its height

   .   .   .   .   .   .

   We should not call those years a waste,
     Which led us to the light.[71]

A sacred burden is this life ye bear; Look on it, lift it, bear it solemnly; Stand up, and walk beneath it steadfastly; Fail not for sorrow, falter not for sin, But Onward! Upward! Till the goal ye win.[72]

Sure, this world is full of trouble—
   I ain't said it ain't.
Lord! I've had enough, an' double,
   Reason for complaint.
Rain an' storm have come to fret me,
   Skies were often gray;
Thorns an' brambles have beset me
   On the road—but, *say*,
   AIN'T IT FINE TODAY?

What's the use of always weeping
   Makin' trouble last?
What's the use of always keepin'
   Thinkin' of the past?
Each must have his tribulation,
   Water with his wine. - -
Life it ain't no celebration.
   Trouble? I've had mine—
   BUT TODAY IS FINE?

It's *today* that I am livin',
   Not a month ago,
Havin', losin', takin', givin',
   As time wills it, so.
Yesterday a cloud of sorrow
   Fell across the way;
It may rain again to-morrow,
   It may rain—but, SAY,
   AIN'T IT FINE TODAY?[73]

Fate used me meanly; but I looked at her and LAUGHED,
That none might know how bitter was the cup I quaffed.
Along came Joy, and paused beside me where I sat,
Saying, "I CAME TO SEE WHAT YOU WERE LAUGHING AT."[74]

When things go wrong:
>   I count it best, when things go wrong,
>   *To hum a tune and sing a song;*
>   A heavy heart means sure defeat,
>   But joy is victory replete,

>   .   .   .   .

>   When things go wrong, remember then
>   The HAPPY *heart has strength of ten;*
>   Forget the sorrow, sing a song—
>   It makes all right when things seem wrong.[75]

Press on! Surmount the rocky steps, Climb boldly o'er the torrent's arch; He fails alone who feebly creeps, He wins who dares the hero's march. Be thou a hero! Let thy might Tramp on eternal snows its way, And through the ebon walls of night Hew down a passage unto day.[76]

>   The Spring blew trumpets of color;
>   Her Green sang in my brain—
>   I heard a blind man groping
>   "Tap—tap" with his cane;
>   I pitied him in his blindness;
>   But can I boast, "I see"?
>   Perhaps there walks a spirit
>   Close by, who pities me,—

>   A spirit who hears me tapping
>   The five-sensed cane of mind
>   Amid such unguessed glories—
>   That I am worse than blind.[77a]

Stick to your aim; the *mongrel's* hold will *slip,*
But only crowbars loose the *bull-dog's* grip.
Small though he looks, the jaw that never yields
Drags down the bellowing monarch of the fields.[77b]

It is easy enough to be pleasant, when life flows by like a song, but the man worth while is one who will smile, when everything goes dead wrong. For the TEST OF THE HEART IS TROUBLE, and it ALWAYS COMES WITH THE YEARS, and the smile that is worth the praises of earth, is the smile that shines through tears.

It is easy enough to be prudent, when nothing tempts you to stray, when without or within no voice of sin is luring your soul away; *but it's only a negative virtue until it is tried by fire,* and the life that is worth the honor on earth, is the one that resists desire.

By the cynic, the sad, the fallen, who had no strength for the strife, the world's highway is cumbered to-day, they make up the sum of life. But the virtue that conquers passion, and the sorrow that hides in a smile, it is these that are worth the homage on earth for we find them but once in a while.[78]

Lives of great men all remind us We can make our life sublime, And, departing, leave behind us Footprints on the sands of time;—   Footprints, that perhaps another, sailing o'er life's solemn main, A forlorn and shipwrecked brother, Seeing, shall take heart again.

Let us then be up and doing, With a heart for any fate; Still achieving, still pursuing, Learn to labor and to wait.[79]

I used to think, when I was small, that all I need to do
To be a man, was just grow up. That was before I knew
So much of grown-up males who lack as much that man-
      hood needs
As when they were but juveniles and dreamed of manly
      deeds
So I have learned this much, at least, since when my life
      began;
It takes much more than growing up to be a real man.

"When I grow up and be a man," you hear the small boys
    say,
As if by merely growing large they should be men some day.
But, knowing manhood's requisites in larger sense, they'll
    learn
There's much besides their body growth for which they
    ought to yearn.
The stately St. Bernard is more than just a larger pup—
It takes much more to be a man, than just a-growing up.

Fine breadth of vision, *self control*, a boundless charity,
A gentler tongue, a stronger faith, more perfect clarity
In spirit-vision; *patience vast*—more patience still, and more,
Wisdom to know—and to forget—all that has gone before;
Courage to smile though sorrow fill unto its brim your cup—
More is required, to make a man, than merely growing up.[80]

Are not two sparrows sold for a penny? And one of them
shall not fall on the ground without your Father; but the
very hairs of your head are all numbered. Fear ye not therefore; ye are of more value than many sparrows.[81]

When you've fought and lost the battle,
Boy o' mine,
Don't come in with childish prattle,
Boy o' mine,
Come in head erect and grinning,
Fit to make a fresh beginning,
Victory isn't all in winning,
Boy o' mine.

What if luck has broken badly?
Boy o' mine,
Don't tell others of it sadly,
Boy o' mine,

Though it's bitter fruit you've eaten,
That your manly ways can sweeten,
Say "I tried, but I was beaten,"
Boy o' mine.

Don't come back with lame excuses,
Boy o' mine,
Learn the lesson sport produces,
Boy o' mine,
Never mind the breaks which cost it
Or the carelessness which tossed it,
'Tis enough to say, "I lost it,"
Boy o' mine.

Take the failure without whining,
Boy o' mine,
Do no fretting or repining,
Boy o' mine;
Here's the one way, don't mistake it;
To your glory you can make it;
If you'll play the man and take it,
Boy o' mine.[82]

Then, *welcome trial,* sickness, ennui, privations, injustice
. . . all of it can only come, *directed by God's Hand,* and
will wound the soul only in order to *cleanse* some spot
within.[83]

God will allow no suffering, no trial above what you are
able to bear.[84]

If we are slighted, misunderstood, maligned, or perse-
cuted, *what does it matter? These injuries will pass away;*
but the peace and love of God will remain with us forever,
the reward of our faith and patience.[85]

HOW TO BEAR LITTLE WORRIES!

In the first place, *expect them!*[86]

When the heart is heavy, and we suffer from depression or disappointment, how thankful we should be that we still have work and prayer left to comfort us. Occupation forcibly diverts the mind; prayer sweetly soothes the soul.[87]

Pluck wins! It always wins! Though days be slow and nights be dark twixt days that come and go. Still, pluck will win! Its average is sure! HE WINS THE MOST, WHO CAN THE MOST ENDURE! Who faces issues! He who never shirks! Who waits, and watches and who always works.[88]

Nothing is so contagious as enthusiasm. It moves stones, it charms brutes. Enthusiasm is the genius of sincerity, and truth accomplishes no victories without it.[89]

Act as if it were impossible to fail.[90]

The great have a way of conquering fate—

I like the man *who faces what he must*
　　With step triumphant and a heart of cheer;
　　Who fights the daily battle without fear;
Sees his hopes fail, yet keeps unfaltering trust
That God is God; that somehow, true and just
　　His plans work out for mortals; not a tear
　　Is shed when fortune, which the world holds dear,
Falls from his grasp; better, with love, a crust
Than living in dishonor; envies not,
　　Nor loses faith in man; but does his best

Nor ever mourns over his humbler lot,
    But with a smile and words of hope, gives zest
To every toiler; HE ALONE IS GREAT,
WHO by a life heroic, CONQUERS FATE.[91]

Everyday there is an occasion when:

Somebody said that it *couldn't be done,*
    But he with a chuckle replied
That "maybe it couldn't but he would be one
    Who wouldn't say so 'till he'd tried.
So he buckled right in, with a trace of a grin
    On his face. If he worried, he hid it.
He started to sing as he tackled the thing
    That couldn't be done, and he DID it.

Somebody scoffed: "Oh, *you'll never do that,*
    At least no one has ever done it."
But he took off his coat and he took off his hat,
    And the first thing we knew he'd begun it;
With a lift of his chin, and a bit of a grin,
    Without any doubt or quibbling;
He started to sing as he tackled the thing
    That couldn't be done, and he DID it.

There are thousands to tell you it cannot be done;
    There are thousands to prophesy failure;
There are thousands to point out to us, one by one,
    The dangers that wait to assail you;
But just buckle in with a bit of a grin,
    Then take off your coat and go to it;
Just start in to *sing as you tackle* the thing
    That "cannot be done" and *you'll* DO *it.*[92a]

It's easy to laugh when the battle's fought
  And you know that the victory's won;
Yes, easy to laugh when the prize you sought
  Is yours when the race is run;
But here's to the man who can laugh when the blast
  Of adversity blows; he will conquer at last,
FOR THE HARDEST MAN IN THE WORLD TO BEAT
  IS THE MAN WHO CAN LAUGH IN THE FACE OF DEFEAT.[92b]

I Salute You!

There is nothing I can give you which you have not; but
there is much that, while I cannot give, you can take.

No heaven can come to us unless our hearts find rest in
it today. *Take Heaven.* No peace lies in the future which
is not hidden in this present instant. *Take Peace.* The gloom
of the world is but a shadow; behind it, yet within our reach,
is joy. *Take Joy.*

And so, at this Christmas time, I greet you, with the
prayer that for you, now and forever, the day breaks and
the shadows flee away.[93]

Did you tackle that trouble that came your way
  With a resolute heart and cheerful?
Or hide your face from the light of day
  With a craven soul and fearful?
Oh, a trouble is a ton or a trouble's an ounce,
  Or a trouble is what you make it,
And it isn't the fact that you're hurt that counts,
  But only HOW DID YOU TAKE IT?

You are beaten to earth? Well, well, what's that?
   Come up with a smiling face.
It's nothing against you to fall down flat,
   But to lie there—that's disgrace!
The harder you're thrown, why the higher you bounce
   Be proud of your blackened eye!
It isn't the fact that you're licked that counts:
   It's how did you fight—and why?

And though you be done to the death, what then?
   If you battled the best you could,
If you played your part in the world of men,
   Why, the Critic will call it good.
Death comes with a crawl, or comes with a pounce,
   And whether he's slow or spry,
It isn't the fact that you're dead that counts,
   BUT ONLY HOW DID YOU DIE?[94]

*These lines have vitally helped others. Perhaps some day
you, too, will find them helpful:
Sometime you may have to* WATCH THE THINGS YOU GAVE
     YOUR LIFE TO, BROKEN
AND STOOP AND BUILD THEM UP WITH WORN-OUT TOOLS.

*There may come a time when you will not have a straw to
cling to except these words. These thoughts should "pull
you through" anything if you remember them, knowing
others have been in impossible situations before you.*

IF YOU CAN FORCE YOUR HEART AND NERVE AND SINEW
   TO SERVE YOUR TURN LONG AFTER THEY ARE GONE
AND SO HOLD ON WHEN THERE'S NOTHING IN YOU
   EXCEPT THE WILL WHICH SAYS TO THEM, "HOLD ON."[95]

REFLECTION

Accept disappointments courageously and they become a challenge to greater effort. If ambitions are worth having, they are worth sacrifice. Sometimes the price may seem exorbitant. But one can make a victory out of a defeat.

Miracles still happen to-day. Often they are the results of man's work carried on to the end—and then one step beyond the end, and thus to unseen victory. When one gets to the place that seems impossible to go over or under or around—that is the place that decides victory or defeat. One's ability to persist at that point makes his victory. If he has built strong habits of persistence and of mental discipline, he succeeds by virtue of his past endeavors. If he has not prepared himself to prevent a crisis should it arise, he is defeated. A man's ability to stick beyond the endurance point brings him in touch with the mystic genius which bridges the chasm from failure to success.

4 THE PURPOSE OF SORROW AND HOW TO MEET IT COURAGEOUSLY

Without experiencing sorrow we cannot fully experience joy. We must have the contrasts of sorrow and joy to help us gain perspective; they give us a knowledge of true values and just proportions. We cannot, by ourselves, climb to greater spiritual knowledge. We must have something which compels us to climb higher. Unless we have learned to conquer ourselves, our environment, and our experiences—we cannot win Life itself! Sorrows give us the stimulus to reach those heights. They compel us to climb up to our utmost Ability. The deeper our sorrows, the greater the heights we can attain if we accept them with understanding and use them:

> "The soul would have no rainbow
> Had the eyes no tears."[1]

Sooner or later all of us come to the "Red Sea" place in life:

Have you come to the *Red Sea place* in your life,
Where in spite of all you can do,
There is NO WAY OUT, there is NO WAY BACK,
There is *no other way but*—THROUGH?

Then wait on the Lord with trust serene,
Till the night of fear is gone;
He will send the wind; He will keep the floods,
When He says to your soul, "GO ON!"[2]

> Must Jesus bear the cross alone,
> And all the world go free?
> No! There's *a cross* for EVERYONE,
> And there's a cross for ME.[3]

The Lord is my Shepherd. I shall not want.[4]

All those who journey, soon or late, must pass within the Garden's gate; must kneel *alone* in darkness there, and battle with some *fierce despair*. God pity those who cannot say: "*Not mine but thine*"; who only pray: "Let this cup pass" and cannot see *the purpose* in Gethsemane.[5]

I for *thy sake* was pierced with heavy sorrow, and bore the cross, Yet heeded not the sharpness of the arrow, nor shame and loss.

So faint not thou, whate'er the burden be, but *bear it bravely, even to Calvary.*[6]

Is life worth living? Aye! With the best of us, heights of us, depths of us, *Life* is the *test of us!*[7]

'Tis the *set of the Soul* that decides the Goal and not the storms of Life.[8]

Little Lady, just remember, Every year has its December, Every rising sun its setting *Every life its time* of fretting.[9]

We know that Heaven chastens those whom it loves best; being pleased, by repeated trials, to make . . . pure spirits more pure.[10]

And when God, who sees all and who wishes to *save us*, upsets our designs, we stupidly complain against Him, we accuse His Providence. We do not comprehend that in punishing us, *in overturning our plans* and causing us suffering, He is *doing all this to deliver us, to open the Infinite to us.*[11]

Now I want you to think that in life troubles will come, which seem as if they never would pass away. The night and storm look as if they would last forever; but the calm and the morning cannot be stayed; the storm in its very nature is transient. The effort of nature, as that of the human heart, ever is to return to its repose, for God is Peace.[12]

DISAPPOINTMENTS ARE SHAFTS sent to the very bottom of our souls, and WHATEVER IS THERE, whether gold, or only copper, THEY BRING IT TO THE SURFACE.[13]

God does not take away trials or carry us over them, but strengthens us through them.[14]

To dare is great. To bear is greater. *Bravery* we share with *brutes. Fortitude* with *saints.*[15]

> The day is cold, and dark, and dreary;
> It rains, and the wind is never weary;
> The vine still clings to the mouldering wall,
> But at every gust the dead leaves fall,
> And the day is dark and dreary.

> My life is cold, and dark, and dreary;
> It rains, and the wind is never weary;
> My thoughts still cling to the mouldering Past,
> But the hopes of youth fall thick in the blast
> And the days are dark and dreary.

Be still, sad heart! and cease repining;
Behind the clouds is the sun still shining;
Thy fate is the common fate of all,
Into each life some rain must fall
    Some days *must be* dark and dreary.[16]

If all the skies were sunshine, our faces would be fain
To feel once more upon them the cooling splash of rain.
If all the world were music, our hearts would often long
for one sweet strain of silence, to break the endless song.
If life were always merry, our souls would seek relief,
And rest from weary laughter in the quiet arms of grief.[17]

Talents are best nurtured in solitude; character is best
formed in the stormy billows of the world.[18]

No cloud can overshadow a true Christian, but his faith
will discern a rainbow.[19]

    For all your days prepare,
      And meet them each alike;
    When you are the anvil, *bear*—
      When you are the hammer, *strike*.[20]

A sorrow comes upon you. . . Meet the dreadful hour
with prayer, cast your care on God, claim Him as your
Father,—and the degrading, paralyzing, embittering effects
of pain and sorrow pass away, a stream of sanctifying and
softening thought pours into the soul, and that which might
have wrought your fall but works in you the peaceful fruits
of righteousness.[21]

    When the pain of bitter bereavement
      Has filled another with grief,

You wish that a portion of comfort
  Might bring him needed relief,

But never a word do you utter
  To lighten the sky that is bleak,
It is well enough that you pity,
  But, brother, *why don't you speak?*[22]

The nurse of full-grown souls is solitude.[23]

*Strange as it may seem, the cruelest blows in life often come
to us from those who are nearest and dearest. Do not let
these heartbreaks overcome you, but rather, overcome the
heartbreaks. They come to all.*

  Life is duty—dare it;
  Life is a burden—bear it;
  Life is a thorn-crown—wear it;
  Though it break thy heart in twain,
  Though the burden bear thee down,
  Close thy lips and stand the pain,
  First the CROSS, and *then* the CROWN.[24]

He that taketh not his cross, and followeth after me, *is not
worthy of me.*[25]

I learn, as the years roll onward and I leave the past behind, that *much I had counted sorrow* but *proved that God
is kind;* that many a flower I'd longed for had hidden a thorn
of pain, and many a rugged by-path led to fields of ripened
grain.

The clouds that cover the sunshine; they cannot banish
the sun. And the earth shines out the brighter when the

weary rain is done. We must stand in the deepest shadow
To see the clearest light; and often *through Wrong's own
darkness Comes* the welcome *strength of Right.*[26]

> The stranger wandering in the Switzer's land,
>   Before its awful mountain tops afraid—
> Who yet, with patient toil, hath gained his stand,
>   On the bare summit where all life is stayed.
>
> Sees far, far down, beneath his blood-dimmed eyes,
>   Another country, golden to the shore,
> Where a new passion and new hopes arise,
>   Where Southern blooms unfold forevermore.
>
> And I, lone sitting by the twilight blaze,
>   Think of another wanderer in the snows,
> And on more perilous mountain-tops I gaze,
>   Than ever frowned above the vine and rose.
>
> Yet courage, soul, nor hold thy strength in vain,
>   In hope *o'ercome the steeps God set for thee;*
> *For past the Alpine summits of great pain*
>   *Lieth thine Italy.*[27]

He that findeth his life, shall lose it; and he that loseth his
life for my sake, shall find it.[28]

Amid my list of blessings infinite, Stands this the fore-
most, That MY HEART HAS BLED.[29]

A Christian man's life is lain in the loom of time, to a pattern which he does not see, *but God does;* and his heart is in
the shuttle. *On one side of the loom is sorrow, and on the
other is joy;* and the shuttle, struck alternately by each, flies

back and forth, carrying the thread, which is white or black as the pattern needs; and in the end, when God shall lift up the finished garment, and all its changing hues shall glance out, it will then appear that the *dark and deep colors were as needful to beauty as the bright and high ones.*[30]

> The hours I spent with thee, dear heart,
>   Are as a string of pearls to me;
> I count them over—every one apart—
>   My rosary, my rosary.

> Each hour a pearl, each pearl a prayer;
>   To still a heart in absence wrung;
> I tell each bead unto the end,
>   And there, a cross is hung!

> Oh, memories that bless and burn,
>   O barren gain, and bitter loss,
> I kiss each bead, and strive at last to learn,
>   Sweetheart, to kiss the cross.[31]

Father, I thank Thee for Thy *mercies* which are new every morning. For the gift of *sleep*; for *health* and *strength*; for the *vision* of another day with its fresh opportunities for work and service; for all these and more than these, I thank Thee. Before looking on the face of men I would look on Thee, who art the health of my countenance and my God. Not without Thy guidance would I go forth to meet the duties and tasks of the day. Strengthen me so that in all my work I may be faithful, amid trials; in suffering, patient; under disappointment, full of hope in Thee. Grant this for Thy goodness' sake. Amen.[32]

BE STRONG!
We are not here to play, to dream, to drift;
We have hard work to do, and loads to lift;
Shun not the struggle—face it; 'tis God's gift.

. . . . . .

BE STRONG!
It matters not how deep intrenched the wrong,
How hard the battle goes, the day how long;
Faint not—fight on! Tomorrow comes the song.[33]

Count each affliction, whether light or grave,
God's messenger sent down to thee; . . . .
. . . . . . Grief should be,
Like joy, majestic, equable, sedate;

Confirming, cleansing, raising, making free;
Strong to consume small troubles; to command
Great thoughts, grave thoughts, thoughts lasting
        to the end.[34]

"Sorrows humanize our race;" because:

Tears are the showers that fertilize this world; And memory of things precious keepeth warm The heart that once did hold them.

They are poor that have lost nothing: They are poorer far Who, losing, have forgotten: They *most poor* of all, *who lose and wish they might forget.*[35]

Not in the time of pleasure Hope doth set her bow; But in the sky of sorrow, Over the vale of woe.

Through gloom and shadow look we On beyond the years; *The soul would have no rainbow Had the eyes no tears.*[36]

O heart of mine WE SHOULDN'T WORRY SO!
What we've missed of calm, we couldn't have, you know!
What we've met of stormy pain and of sorrow's drifting rain.
WE CAN BETTER MEET AGAIN, if it blow!

We have erred in that dark hour we have known,
When our tears fell with the shower all alone!
Were not shine and sorrows blent
As our Gracious Master meant?
Let us temper our content with his own
For we know not ev'ry morrow can be sad
So, forgetting all the sorrow we have had
Let us fold away our fears
And put away our foolish tears
And through all the coming years just be glad
        Just be Glad![37]

I have known sorrow—therefore I
May laugh with you, O friend more merrily
Than those who never sorrowed upon earth
And know not laughter's worth.

I have known laughter—therefore I
May sorrow with you far more tenderly
Than those who never guess how sad a thing
Seems merriment to one's heart's suffering.[38]

I thank Thee, Lord, for mine unanswered prayers, unanswered save Thy quiet, kindly "Nay." Yet it seemed hard among my heavy cares That bitter day.
I wanted joy; but Thou didst know for me that sorrow was the gift I needed most, and in its mystic depth *I learned to see the Holy Ghost.* I wanted health; but Thou didst bid me sound the secret treasuries of pain, And in the moans

and groans *my heart oft found Thy Christ again.* I
wanted wealth; 'twas not the better part; there is a wealth
with poverty oft given, and Thou didst teach me of the gold
of heart, best gift of heaven.

I thank Thee, Lord, for these unanswered prayers, and
for Thy word, the quiet kindly "Nay." 'Twas Thy withhold-
ing lightened all my cares that blessed day.[39]

> When God at first made man,
> Having a glass of blessings standing by;
>   "Let us," said He, "pour on him all we can;
> Let the world's riches, which dispersed lie,
>   Contract into a span."
>
> So Strength first made a way;
> Then Beauty flowed; then Wisdom, Honor, Pleasure.
>   When almost all was out, God made a stay,
> Perceiving that alone, of all His treasure,
>   *Rest* in the bottom lay.
>
> "For if I should," said He,
> "Bestow this jewel also on My creature,
>   *He would adore My gifts instead of Me,*
> *And rest in Nature, not the God of Nature;*
>   So both should losers be.
>
> Yet let him keep the rest
> But *keep them with repining restlessness;*
>   Let him be rich and weary, that at least,
> *If goodness lead him not, yet weariness*
>   May toss him to My breast."[40]
>
> A mighty monarch in the days of old
> Made offer of high honor, wealth and gold,

To one who should produce in form concise
A motto for his guidance, terse, yet wise;
A precept soothing in his hours forlorn,
Yet one that in his prosperous days should warn.
Many the maxims sent the king, men say;
The one he chose, "This, too, shall pass away."

Has some misfortune fallen to *your* lot?
This, too, will pass away; absorb the thought,
And wait—your waiting will not be in vain,
Time gilds with gold the iron links of pain.
The dark today leads into light tomorrow;
There is no endless joy, no endless sorrow.

Are *you upon earth's heights, no cloud in view?*
Go read your motto once again, *"This, too,
Shall pass away."* Fame, glory, and power,
They are but little bubbles of the hour,
Flung by the ruthless years down in the dust.
Take warning and *be worthy of God's trust.*

Use well your prowess while it lasts; leave bloom,
Not blight, to mark your footprints to the tomb;
The truest *greatness lies in being kind,*
The truest *wisdom is a happy mind.*
He who desponds, his Maker's judgement mocks,
The gloomy Christian is a paradox.

Only the sunny soul respects its God.
Since life is brief, we need to make it broad;
Since life is short, we need to make it bright;
Thus keep the old king's motto well in sight,
And let its meaning permeate each day
Whatever comes—"THIS, TOO, SHALL PASS AWAY."[41]

After pain consider—

> What if this year has given
>   Grief that some year must bring,
> What if it hurt your *joyous youth,*
>   Crippled your laughter's wing?
> You always knew it was coming,
>   *Coming to all,* to you,
> They always said there was suffering—
>   *Now it is done,* come through!

. . . . . .

> Only your heart can pity
>   Now, where it laughed and passed,
> Now you can bend to comfort men,
>   *One with them all at last,*
> You shall have back your laughter,
>   You shall have back your song,
> Only *the world is your brother* now,
>   Only *your soul is strong.*[42]

> In the cross of Christ I glory,
>   Towering o'er the wrecks of time:
> All the light of sacred story
>   Gathers round its head sublime.

> When the woes of life o'ertake me,
>   Hopes deceive and fears annoy,
> Never shall the cross forsake me:
>   Low, it glows with peace and joy.

> When the sun of bliss is beaming
>   Light and love upon my way,

From the cross the radiance streaming
   Adds more luster to the day.

Bane and blessing, *pain and pleasure,*
   By the cross are sanctified:
Peace there is that knows no measure,
   Joys that through all time abide.

   In the cross of Christ I glory,
      Towering o'er the wrecks of time;
   All the light of sacred story
      Gathers round its head sublime.[43]

Abide with me! Fast falls the eventide,
The darkness deepens; Lord, with me abide!
When other helpers fail, and comforts flee,
Help of the helpless, O, abide with me!

Swift to its close ebbs out life's little day;
Earth's joys grow dim, its glories pass away;
Change and decay in all around I see;
O Thou, who changest not, abide with me!

I need thy presence every passing hour;
What but thy grace can foil the tempter's power?
Who, like thyself, my guide and stay can be?
Through cloud and sunshine, Lord, abide with me.

I fear no foe, with thee at hand to bless;
Ills have no weight, and tears no bitterness;
Where is death's sting? Where, grave, thy victory?
I triumph still, if thou abide with me!

Hold Thou Thy cross before my closing eyes;
Shine through the gloom and point me to the skies;
Heaven's morning breaks, and earth's vain shadows flee
In life, in death, O Lord, abide with me![44]

THE POWERS OF THE SOUL ARE COMMENSURATE WITH ITS
NEEDS.[45]

O Master, let me walk with Thee in lowly paths of service free; tell me Thy secret; *help me bear the strain of toil,
the fret of care.*

Help me the slow of heart to move by some clear winning word of love, teach me the wayward feet to stay, and
guide them in the homeward way.

Teach me Thy patience; still with Thee in closer, dearer
company, in work that keeps faith sweet and strong, in trust
that triumphs over wrong.

In hope that sends a shining ray Far down the future's
broadening way, *In peace that only Thou canst give,* With
Thee, O Master, let me live.[46]

When a loved one dies:

> *He is made one with Nature;* there is heard
> His voice in all her music, from the moan
> Of Thunder, to the song of night's sweet bird;
> *He is a presence to be felt and known*
> In darkness and in light, from herb and stone,
> Spreading itself where'er that Power may move
> Which has withdrawn His being to its own;
> Which wields the world with never-wearied love,
> Sustains it from beneath, and kindles it above.
>
> *He is a portion of the loveliness*
> *Which once he made more lovely;*[47]

Those we love truly never die,
Though year by year the sad memorial wreath,
A ring and flowers, types of life and death,
　　Are laid upon their graves.

For death the pure life saves,
And life all pure is love; and LOVE CAN REACH
FROM HEAVEN TO EARTH, and nobler lessons teach
　　Than those by mortals read.

Well blest is he who has a dear one dead;
A friend he has whose *face will never change—*
A dear communion that will not grow strange;
THE ANCHOR OF A LOVE IS DEATH.[48]

Do not come when I am dead to sit beside a low green mound, or bring the first gay daffodils because I love them so, for *I shall not be there,* You cannot find me *there.*

I will look up at you from the eyes of little children; I will bend to meet you in the swaying boughs of bud-thrilled trees and caress you with the passionate sweep of storm filled winds; *I will give you strength in your upward tread* of everlasting hills; I will cool your tired body in the flow of the limpid river; I will warm your work-glorified hands through the glow of the winter fire; I will soothe you into forgetfulness to the drop, drop of the rain on the roof; I will speak to you, out of the rhymes of the Masters: I will dance with you in the lilt of the violin, and make your heart leap with the bursting cadence of the organ: I will flood your soul with the flaming radiance of the sunrise, and bring you peace in the tender rose and gold of the after-sunset.

All these have made me happy; They are a part of me: I shall become a part of them.[49]

I thought our love at full, but I did err; joy's wreath
drooped o'er mine eyes; I could not see *that sorrow in our
happy world must be Love's deepest spokesman* and inter-
preter:

But, as a mother feels her child first stir under her heart,
so felt I instantly deep in my soul another bond to thee
thrill with that life we saw depart from her; O mother of
our angel child! *twice dear!*
DEATH KNITS AS WELL AS PARTS, and still, I wish
Her tender radiance shall infold us here.[50]

To make undying music in the world, Breathing a beauteous order, that controls With growing sway the growing
life of man. *May I reach that purest heaven,—be to other
souls the cup of strength in some great agony,* Enkindle
generous ardor, feed pure love, Beget the smiles that have
no cruelty, Be the sweet presence of a good diffused, And
in diffusion ever more intense, *So shall I join the choir invisible, Whose music is the gladness of the world.*[51]

Lead, kindly light, amid the encircling gloom,
        LEAD THOU ME ON!
The night is dark and I am far from home:
        LEAD THOU ME ON!
Keep thou my feet; I do not ask to see
The distant scene: *one step enough for me.*

I was not ever thus, nor prayed that thou
        Shouldst lead me on:
I loved to choose and see my path; BUT NOW
        Lead thou me on.
I loved the garish day, and, spite of fears
Pride ruled my will: remember not past years!

So long Thy power hath blest me, sure it still
    Will lead me on
O'er moor and fen, o'er crag and torrent, till
    The night is gone:
And with the morn those angel faces smile,
Which I have loved long since, and lost awhile.[52]

    O Love, that wilt not let me go,
      I rest my weary soul on Thee;
    I give Thee back the life I owe,
    That in Thine ocean depth its flow
      May richer, fuller be.

    O Light, that followest all my way,
      I yield my flickering torch to Thee;
    My heart restores its borrowed ray,
    That in Thy sunshine's blaze its day
      May brighter, fairer be.

    O Joy, that seekest me through pain,
      I cannot close my heart to Thee;
    I trace the rainbow through the rain,
    And feel the promise is not vain,
      That morn shall tearless be.

    O Cross, that liftest up my head,
      I dare not ask to fly from Thee;
    I lay in dust life's glory dead,
    And from the ground there blossoms red
      Life that shall endless be.[53]

Mysterious night. When our first parent knew
Thee from report divine, and heard thy name,
Did he not tremble for this lovely frame,
This glorious canopy of light and blue,

Yet 'neath the curtain of translucent dew,
Bathed in the rays of the great setting flame,
Hesperus with the host of heaven came,
And lo! *Creation widened on man's view.*
Who could have thought such darkness lay concealed
Within thy beams, O sun! or who could find
While fly, and leaf, and insect stood revealed,
That to such countless orbs thou made us blind.
Why do we, then, shun Death with anxious strife?—
  If Light can thus deceive, wherefore not Life?[54]

A HEARTBREAK is a little thing,
  It only means that you
Will have no foolish songs to sing
  Nor useless things to do.

A heartbreak means that you can sit
  And watch a dream go by,
And laugh because you know that it
Will sicken soon, and die.

So small a thing, a heartbreak is,
  There is no word or touch,
No hand you clasp or smile you miss,
Can move you very much.

A heartbreak means that where a kiss
  Has dealt you pain before,
There is no thing—next world or this—
  Can hurt you any more.[55]

I walked a mile with *pleasure,*
She chatted all the way
But left me none the wiser
For all she had to say.

I walked a mile with sorrow
And never a word said she
But Oh! The things I learned from her
When sorrow walked with me.[56]

Sometime when all life's lessons have been learned,
  And Sun and Moon and Stars forevermore have set,
The things which our weak judgements here have spurned,
  The things o'er which we grieved with lashes wet,
Will flash before us out of life's dark night
  As stars shine most in deeper tints of blue;
And we shall see how all God's plans were right
  And how *what seemed reproof was love most true.*

  And we shall see, how, while we frown and sigh,
    God's plans go on as best for you and me;
  How when we called, *he heeded not our cry,*
    Because his wisdom to the end could see,
  And even as prudent parents disallow
    Too much of sweet to craving babyhood,
  So God, perhaps, is keeping from us now
    Life's sweetest things, because it seemeth good.

And if, sometimes, commingled with life's wine,
  We find the wormwood, and rebel and shrink,
Be sure a wiser hand than yours and mine
  Pours out this potion for our lips to drink
And if someone we love is lying low,
  Where human kisses cannot reach the face,
Oh, do not blame the loving Father so,
  But wear your sorrow with obedient grace.

  And you will shortly know that *lengthened breath*
    Is not the sweetest gift God gives His friends;

And that, sometimes, *the sable pall of death*
   Conceals the fairest boon His love can send.
If we could push ajar the gates of life,
   And stand within, and all God's workings see,
We could interpret all this doubt and strife,
   And for each mystery could find a key.

But not today. Then be content, poor heart,
  God's plan like lilies, pure and white, unfold;
We must not tear the close-shut leaves apart:
  Time will reveal the calyxes of gold,
And if, through patient toil, we reach the land
  Where tired feet, with sandals loosed may rest,
When we shall clearly know and understand,
  I think that we will say, *"God knew the best."*[57]

  "Good-night, sleep well." we say to those we love,
    And watch dear faces glimmer on the stair,
    And hear faint footfalls in the rooms above
      Sound on the quiet air,
    Yet feel no fear, though lonely they must go
    The road of slumber's strange oblivion:
      Dark always wears to dawn,
    Sleep is so gentle, and so well we know,
      Wherever they have gone,
    They will be safe until the morning light,
      Good-night, good-night.

Good-night, sleep well, beloveds, when the last
Slow dusk has fallen, and your steps no more
Make music on the empty upper floor,
   And day is fully past.
We who so lightly let you go alone,
Evening by evening, from our trustful sight

Into the mystery of sleep's unknown—
  We need not fear, tonight,
Death is so gentle—dark will break at dawn . . .
Love will be safe until the morning light.
  Sleep well, good-night![58]

    Life, I challenge you to try me,
      Doom me to unending pain;
    Stay my hand, becloud my vision,
      Break my heart and then—again.

    Shatter every dream I've cherished,
      Fill my heart with ruthless fear;
    Follow every smile that cheers me
      With a bitter, blinding tear.

    Thus I dare you; you can try me,
      Seek to make me cringe and moan,
    Still my unbound soul defies you,
      I'll withstand you—and alone![59]

Our crosses are hewn from different trees,
But we *all must have our calvaries;*
We may climb the height from a *different side,*
But we *each go up* to be crucified;
As we scale the steep, another may share
The dreadful load that our shoulders bear,
But the costliest sorrow is *all our own*—
For on the summit we bleed *alone.*[60]

The loss of a mother may well mean—

    Now there shall be a new song and a new star,
      A new voice in the wind to whisper me;

And I shall stand within the harbor bar
  And watch a new light tossing down the sea.

My childish terror of the Lord shall cease;
  And my dread fear of blind and horrid fate;
And from my sin I shall have sure release
  Because in heaven She is my advocate.[61]

We can yet triumph. We have tried and fail'd
And tried again and fail'd again and tried.
Many a time I've wished that I had died
Before I saw the light. But though I quail'd,
Yet have I stubbornly my fate assail'd
With dazed determination, dignified
With prayer and gratitude, and always cried
"Thy will be done, O God." And God prevailed.[62]

REFLECTION

*Disappointment and sorrow come to all. There is no new
individual experience in Life. Sometimes we think our troubles, our sorrows, our crosses, our experiences are the ex-
ceptional, but sooner or later we find a parallel case. Others
have had the same troubles and found an honorable solution
to them. It is encouraging to know that we are not treading
a new, untried road. As we journey through the maze of
life, we are walking hand-in-hand with all humanity, laughing and sorrowing, not alone, but with all others. We could
not rise if we had nothing to rise above. We could not overcome sin or sorrow if we had no sin or sorrow to overcome.
Overcoming trouble and sorrow is the only way to develop
power. To gain fame, wealth, or spirituality one has to be
tried and found "not wanting" in courage or in persistence.
    Nearly two thousand years ago a man named Jesus, walked*

the path of Life on earth. He lived and suffered as we now do and died while he was still a young man—33. One of His best friends betrayed him as our friends sometimes betray us and Jesus had to tread the narrow, rugged path to Calvary bearing his own cross which weighed unmercifully on him. Yet he bore it bravely to the hill-top and on the summit he bled alone. Humanly he looked for friendship to sustain Him, but none of His friends helped Him. They could not, even if they had so desired. Christ had no one on whom to depend. His faith alone carried him through.

Is it not the greatest of human conceits to lament the fact that sorrow and suffering should come to us? Often we feel unjustly punished and think we have had more than our share of trouble. We cry out, "Why should such a calamity fall upon me?" Should we not rather ask ourselves, "Why shouldn't such a thing befall me?" "Am I so much better than Christ that I can expect to escape those things which He was compelled to accept?"

And so must we come to our Calvary: alone. There is no human power to help. It is then that we face God stripped of all material falseness. And on the summit we bleed alone.

Surely that which was best for Christ is best for us. Those who would follow in His footsteps find the way is still dark and dreary. There are still heavy crosses to be borne, unbearable seemingly—beyond human power to lift, but "This too shall Pass Away!" Each cross, each trouble has its little day and then it passes away. When we finally accept our Cross and bear it bravely, we live in Christ, our rock and our salvation.

Sorrow is sacred—often it is the fairest boon His love can send. It is an experience in Life without which we cannot fully understand the meaning of Easter, and the Resurrection. Without it we cannot reach perfect happiness and contentment.

5 DEFINITE LAWS CONTROL
FRIENDSHIP

If we would receive the affection and respect of friends, we must give these things to others. "To have a friend, you must be a friend."

"A man that hath friends must show himself friendly."[1]

To know all is to forgive all—

> If I knew you and you knew me,
>   If both of us could clearly see
> And with an inner sight divine
>   The meaning of your heart and mine
> I'm sure that we should differ less
>   And clasp our hands in friendliness.
>
> If I knew you and you knew me,
>   As each one knows his own self, we
> Could look each other in the face
>   And see therein a truer grace.
> Life has so many hidden woes,
>   So many thorns for every rose;
> The "why" of things our hearts would see,
>   If I knew you and you knew me.[2]

If your friend is a help, a joy, an inspiration to you, *tell him so*. There are discouraged hearts everywhere just hungry for appreciation and sympathy.[3]

Seek close by first:

No one could tell me where my soul might be;
I searched for God, and He eluded me;
I sought my brother out, and FOUND ALL THREE.[4]

We judge men by our own standards; judge our nearest and dearest often wrong.[5]

If you are depressed because some of your acquaintances seem jealous and unappreciative you should realize that life has always been so. Greater men than you have suffered thus and proved their greatness by the way they rose above such petty concerns.
Next time you think "I just can't stand that person," stop and realize that the thing you dislike is a human fault, grown out of proportion. Until you can be certain that you have no such marring faults, suspend judgement. Forgive your enemy for he knows not what he does. In doing evil to another he brings evil upon himself.

If words of thine have cheered one failing heart,
  Kindled anew one fading altar fire,
Thy work is not a failure; chords are touched
  That shall re-echo from the angel choir.[6]

Believe not each accusing tongue,
  As most weak persons do;
But still believe that sorry wrong
  Which ought not to be true.[7]

If you hear a kind word spoken
  Of some worthy soul you know,
It may fill his heart with sunshine
  If you only *tell him so.*

If a deed, however humble,
  Helps you on your way to go,
Seek the one whose hand has helped you,
  Seek him out and tell him so![8]

"A friend in need," my neighbor said to me;
"A friend in need, is what I mean to be.
In time of trouble I will come to you,
And in the hour of need you'll find me true."

I thought a bit, then took him by the hand;
"My friend," I said, "you do not understand
The inner meaning of that simple rhyme;
A friend is what *the heart needs all the time.*"[9]

The time for kindness is NOW.

    Friends, in this world of hurry
    And work and sudden end
    If a thought comes quick of doing
    A kindness to a friend
    Do it this very instant!
    Don't put it off—don't wait;
    What's the use of doing a kindness
    If you do it a day too late?[10]

What a strange idea we sometimes have that love gives us
the privilege of rudeness. Show your friend who so easily
overlooks your faults the same fine courtesy that you show
a stranger who would not overlook them."[11]

    There is a destiny that makes us brothers;
      None goes his way alone;
    All that we send into the lives of others
      Comes back into our own.[12]

Youth, beauty, graceful action, seldom fail, but common interest always will prevail.[13]

But if ye do not forgive, neither will your Father which is in heaven forgive your trespasses.[14]

HE WHO HARBORS A SLIGHT WILL MISS THE HAVEN OF HAPPINESS.[15]

Two persons will not be friends long if they cannot forgive each other's failings.[16]

> GIVE TO THE WORLD THE BEST THAT YOU HAVE,
> AND THE BEST WILL COME BACK TO YOU.
> Give Love, and Love to your heart will flow,
> A strength in your utmost need.
> Have faith, and a score of hearts will show
> Their faith in your work and deed.[17]

Judge not, because THOU CANST NOT JUDGE ARIGHT. Not much thou know'st thyself, yet better far than thou know'st others. Language is at war with purposes; appearances must fight.[18]

To thine own self be true, And it must follow, as the night the day, Thou canst not then be false to any man.[19]

Protect your friends.

> If you are tempted to reveal
> A tale to you someone has told
> About another, make it pass,
> Before you speak, three gates of God.
> These narrow gates: First, *"Is it true?"*
> Then, *"Is it needful?"* In your mind

Give truthful answer. And the next
Is last and narrowest, "Is it kind?"
And if to reach your lips at last
It passes through these gateways three,
Then you may tell the tale, nor fear
What the result of speech may be.*[20]

There is so much bad in the best of us, And so much good
in the worst of us, That it doesn't behoove any of us To talk
about the rest of us.[21]

I expect to pass through this world but once. Any good
thing, therefore, that I can do, or *any kindness* that I can
show a fellow being, *let me do it now.* Let me not defer or
neglect it, for I shall not pass this way again.[22]

Heat not a furnace for your foe so hot that it do singe
yourself.[23]

Choose your friend wisely,
Test your friend well
True friends, like rarest gems
Prove hard to tell;
Winter him, summer him
Know your friend well.[24]

To my best friends:
Because of your firm faith, I kept the track
Those sharp-set stones my strength had almost spent—

*However don't make the mistake of thinking it is good-sportsmanship
to cover up and protect one who is doing wrong. It is better to uncover
the festering sore and let light and truth cleanse it before it grows to large
proportions. Christ did not close his eyes to evil. Wherever he saw evil,
he exposed it, reprimanded it, and ordered it away. The hypocrites in the
church and the money changers at the church doorway were scourged in
His demand for *truth*.

I could not meet your eyes, if I turned back,
>> So on I went.

Because of your strong love, I held my path
When battered, worn and bleeding in my fight—
How could I meet your true eyes, blazing wrath?
>> So I kept right.[25]

To the special few:
Oh, the comfort—the inexpressible comfort of feeling safe
with a person; having neither to weigh thoughts nor measure words, but pouring them all right out, just as they are,
chaff and grain together; certain that a faithful hand will take
and sift them, keep what is worth keeping, and with a breath
of kindness blow the rest away.[26]

I would be true, for there are those who trust me;
>> I would be pure, for there are those who care;
I would be strong, for there is much to suffer;
>> I would be brave, for there is much to dare.
I would be friend of all—the poor, the friendless;
>> I would be giving and forget the gift.
I would be humble, for I know my weakness;
>> I would look up—and laugh—and love—and lift.[27]

Old friends, old scenes will lovelier be,
As more of Heaven in each we see;
Some softening gleam of love and prayer
Shall dawn on every cross and care.[28]

O, my friend, it would be better
If to those we love, we gave,
Tender words while they were with us,
Than to say them o'er a grave.

> Those who die no longer need them
> And the words they long to know,
> While they live are only wasted
> On the cold deaf ear below.[29]

How few there are who would thus dare to address God each night:—"Lord, deal with me to-morrow as I have this day dealt with others. . . . those to whom I was harsh and, from malice or to show my own superiority, exposed their failings; others to whom from pride or dislike I refused to speak—one I have avoided—another I cannot like because she displeases me—I will not forgive—to whom I will not show any kindness."

And yet, let us never forget, that sooner or later, God will do unto us even as we have done unto them.[30]

Don't ignore friends!

> Around the corner I have a friend,
> In this great city that has no end;
> Yet days go by, and weeks rush on,
> And before I know it a year is gone,
> And I never see my friend's face,
> For life is a swift and terrible race.
> He knows I like him just as well
> As in the days when I rang his bell
> And he rang mine. We were younger then,
> And now we are busy, tired men;
> Tired with playing a foolish game,
> Tired with trying to make a name.
> *"Tomorrow," I say,* "I will call on Jim,
> Just to show that I'm thinking of him."
> But tomorrow comes—and tomorrow goes,
> And the distance between us grows and grows.

Around the corner, yet miles away.
"Here's a telegram, sir,"
    "Jim died today."
And that's what we get, and deserve, in the end:
Around the corner, a vanished friend.[31]

Forget each kindness that you do
    As soon as you have done it,
Forget the praise that falls to you
    The moment you have won it,
Forget the slanders that you hear
    Before you can repeat it,
Forget each slight, each spite, each sneer,
    Wherever you may meet it.

Remember every kindness done
    To you what e'er its measure,
Remember praise by others won
    And pass it on with pleasure,
Remember every promise made
    And keep it to the letter,
Remember those who lend you aid,
    And be a grateful debtor.

Remember all the happiness
    That comes your way in living;
Forget each worry and distress,
    Be hopeful and forgiving,
Remember good, remember truth
    Remember heaven's above you
And you will find through age and youth
    True joys, and hearts to love you.[32]

A gift is as the foal of a camel. It should carry nothing
on its back.[33]

Sometimes, when you're away from home
   And everything seems queer,
And you sort o' keep a list'nin'
   For a word or two of cheer—

Why, it makes you feel like shoutin'
   If folks walk up to you
And treat you kind and friendly—
   When you're feelin' sad and blue.

It don't take much to spur you on
   And keep you in the game;
It may be just a trifle,
   But it helps you just the same.

It may only be a hand-shake,
   Or a pleasant "Howdy-do?"—
But it's worth a lot of money—
   When you're feelin' sad and blue.[34]

The vital power of good example lives on from generation to generation, keeping the world ever fresh and
young.[35]

'Tis the one who's full of sunshine,
   And who genuinely tries,
Who will clear the clouds of trouble
   From his own and other's skies.

    . . . .

Deeds of honest loving-kindness
   Give a fallen fellow heart.
And upon his uphill journey,
   Help him play a manly part.[36]

Let me be a little kinder, let me be a little blinder
To the faults of those about me; let me praise a little more.
Let me be, when I am weary, just a little bit more cheery;
Let me serve a little better those that I am striving for.
Let me be a little braver, when temptation bids me waver;
Let me strive a little harder to be all that I should be.
Let me be a little meeker with the brother that is weaker;
Let me think more of my neighbor and a little less of me.[37]

> O wad some Pow'r the giftie gie us
>   To see oursels as ithers see us!!
> It wad frae mony a blunder free us,
>   And foolish notion:
> What airs in dress an' gait wad lea'e us,
>   And e'en devotion![38]

Keep us O Lord from pettiness; Let us be large in thought,
    in word and deed,
Let us be done with fault finding and leave off self-seeking.
May we put away all pretense and meet each other face to
    face, without self-pity and without prejudice,
May we *never be hasty in judgment,* and always generous.
Teach us to put into action our better impulses, straight-
    forward and unafraid.
Let us take time for all things; make us grow calm, serene,
    gentle,
Grant that we realize that it is the *little things* that *create
    differences.*
That IN THE BIG THINGS OF LIFE WE ARE AS ONE.
And may we strive to touch and know the great common
    human heart of all of us
And, O Lord God, let us not forget to be kind.[39]

> The Holy Supper is kept, indeed,
> In whatsoever *we share* with another's need;

NOT WHAT WE GIVE, but what we SHARE,
For the gift without the giver is bare;
Who gives himself with his alms feeds three,
Himself, his hungering neighbor, and Me.[40]

ALL ARE BUT PARTS OF ONE STUPENDOUS WHOLE.[41]

HE WHO SERVES HIS BROTHER BEST
GETS NEARER GOD THAN ALL THE REST.[42]

Forbearance is even more than forgiveness; it is excusing, putting always the best construction upon everything; above all, never showing that one proceeding has wounded us.[43]

It is a funny thing, but true,
    That *folks you don't like, don't like you.*
I don't know why this should be so,
    But just the same I allus know
If I am "sour", friends are few;
    If I am friendly, folks are too.

Sometimes I get up in the morn
    A-wishin' I was never born.
I make of cross remarks a few,
    And then my family wishes too
That I had gone some other place
    Instead of showin' them my face.

But let me change my little tune
    And sing and smile, then pretty soon
The folks around me sing and smile
    (I guess 'twas catchin' all the while).
Yes, 'tis a funny thing, but true,
    That folks you like will sure like you.[44]

All men have their frailties, and *whosoever looks for a friend without imperfection will never find what he seeks.* We love ourselves notwithstanding our faults, and we ought to love our friends in like manner.[45]

An opal lay in the case, cold and lusterless. It was held a few moments in a warm hand, when it gleamed and glowed with all the beauty of the rainbow. All about us are human lives of children or of older persons, which seem cold and unbeautiful, without spiritual radiance or gleams of indwelling light which tell of immortality. Yet they need only the touch of a warm human hand, the pressure of love, to bring out in them the brightness of the spiritual beauty that is hidden in them.[46]

> If any little word of mine
>   May make a life the brighter,
> If any little song of mine
>   May make a heart the lighter,
> God help me speak the little word,
>   And take my bit of singing,
> And drop it in some lovely vale
>   To set the echoes ringing.
>
> If any little love of mine
>   May make a life the sweeter,
> If any little care of mine
>   May make a friend's the fleeter,
> If any little lift of mine may ease
>   The burden of another,
> God give me love and care and strength
>   To help my toiling brother.[47]

I hope to be false to nothing you have been taught to expect of me.[48]

The test of friendship is its fidelity when every charm of fortune and environment has been spent away, and the bare, undraped character alone remains; if love still holds steadfast, and the joy of companionship survives in such an hour, the fellowship becomes a beautiful prophecy of immortality.[49]

May every soul that touches mine
Be it the slightest contact, *get therefrom some good;*
Some little grace, one kindly thought,
One aspiration yet unfelt, *one bit of courage* for the darkening sky,
One gleam of faith to brave the thickening ills of life,
One glimpse of brighter skies beyond the gathering mists—
To make this life worth while, and heaven a surer heritage.[50]

The only safe and sure way to destroy an enemy is to make him your friend.[51]

Who is thy neighbor? He whom thou
    Hast power to aid or bless;
Whose aching heart or burning brow
    Thy soothing hand may press.

Thy neighbor? Pass no mourner by;
    Perhaps thou canst redeem
A breaking heart from misery;
    Go share thy lot with him.[52]

It is wisely written—A friend turned hostile is the worst enemy.[53]

To make anyone believe himself good is to make him, almost in spite of self, to become so.[54]

6 LOVE

"Give to the world the best that you have, and the best will come back to you."

"There is but one humanity. All are interrelated, parts of one great whole. Aiding a fellow human is merely aiding a small division of one's own larger spiritual self. Hurting another only hurts one's self.

Each individual has some contribution to make to life and to each person he comes in contact with.

"'Tis love That makes the world go round."[1]

Never forget this: A selfish heart desires love for itself— a Christian heart delights to love—without return.

. . . .

The mistake we make, is when we seek to be beloved, instead of loving. What makes us cowardly, is the fear of losing that love.[2]

Sympathy is the safeguard of the human soul against selfishness.[3]

Love is not love which alters when it alteration finds.[4]

"He that loveth not, knoweth not God; for God is love."[5]

There is no fear in love; but perfect love casteth out fear.[6]

And this commandment have we from him, "That he who loveth God love his brother also."[7]

Love worketh no ill to his neighbor; therefore love is the fulfilling of the law.[8]

> Let me but love my love without disguise,
>   Nor wear a mask of fashion old or new,
>   Nor wait to speak till I can hear a clue,
>   Nor play a part to shine in other's eyes,
>   Nor bow my knees to what my heart denies;
> But what I am, to that let me be true,
>   And let me worship where my love is due,
>   And so through love and worship let me rise.[9]

> Love seeketh not itself to please,
>   Nor for itself has any care.
> But for another gives its ease,
>   And builds a heaven in hell's despair.[10]

Faults are thick where love is thin.[11]

What appears at sight Extremely heavy, love will make most light.[12]

A good deed is never lost; he who sows courtesy reaps friendship, and he who plants kindness gathers love.[13]

'Tis easy to be gentle when Death's silence shames our clamor, And easy to discern the best Through memory's mystic glamour; But wise it were for thee and me, Ere love is past forgiving, To take the tender lesson home—Be patient with the living.[14]

I could not love thee, dear, so much loved I not honour
more.[15]

What we can do for another is the test of powers; what
we can suffer for is the test of love.[16]

All that I have I give with love unspoken.
All that I ask—you keep the faith unbroken.[17]

Do you know *you have asked the costliest thing*
   Ever made by the hand above—
A woman's heart, and a woman's life,
   And a woman's wonderful love?

Do you know you have asked for *this priceless thing*
   As a child might ask for a toy—
Demanding what others have died to win,
   With the reckless dash of a boy?

You have written my lesson of duty out,
   Man-like you have questioned me;
Now stand at the bar of my woman's soul
   Until I shall question thee.

You require your mutton shall always be hot,
   Your socks and your shirts shall be whole;
I require your *heart to be true as God's* stars,
   And *pure as* heaven *your soul.*

You require a cook for your mutton and beef;
   I require a far better thing.
A seamstress you're wanting for stockings and shirts;
   I look for a man and a king—

A king for a beautiful realm called home,
   And a man that the Maker, God,
Shall look upon as he did the first,
   And say, "It is very good."

I am fair and young, but the rose will fade
   From my soft, young cheek one day;
Will you love me, then, mid falling leaves,
   As you did 'mid the bloom of May?

Is your heart an ocean so strong and deep,
   I may launch my all on its tide?
A *loving woman finds heaven or hell*
   On the day she is made a bride.

I require all things that are grand and true,
   All things that a man should be;
If you give this all, I would stake my life
   To be all you demand of me.

If you cannot do this—a *laundress and cook*
   You can hire with little to pay;
But a *woman's heart and a woman's life*
   Are *not to be won that way.*[18]

Can you say this—honestly?
  Believe me, if all those endearing young charms,
    Which I gaze on so fondly today,
  Were to change by to-morrow, and fleet in my arms,
    Like fairy gifts, fading away,
  Thou wouldst still be adored, as this moment thou art,
    Let thy loveliness fade as it will,
  And around the dear ruin each wish of my heart
    Would entwine itself verdantly still.

It is not while beauty and youth are thine own,
    And thy cheeks unprofaned by a tear,
That the fervor and faith of a soul can be known
    To which time will but make thee more dear.
No, the heart that has truly loved never forgets,
    But as truly loves on to the close,
As the sun-flower turns on her god, when he sets,
    The same look which she turned when he rose.[19]

*Women often expect their husbands to love them in the way
they love, and husbands expect wives to return the same
type of love they have, but men love differently than
women. Much unhappiness could be avoided if men and
women realized this fact.*

In him it is a *vast devouring flame—*
Resistless fed—*in its own strength* consumed.
In woman's *heart it enters step by step,*
Concealed, disowned, until its gentler ray
Breathes forth a light, illumining her world.
Man loves not for repose; he woos the flower
To wear it as the victor's trophied crown;
Whilest woman, when she glories in her love,
More like the dove, *in noiseless constancy,*
Watches the nest of her affection till
'Tis shed upon the tomb of him she loves.

The woman's cause is man's; *they rise or sink*
Together, dwarf'd or godlike, bound or free;
For she that out of Lethe scales with man
The shining steps of Nature, shares with man
His nights, his days, moves with him to one goal,
Stays all this fair young planet in her hands—
If she be small, slight-natured, miserable,

How shall men grow? but work no more alone!
Our place is much; as far as in us lies
We two will serve them both in aiding her—
Will clear away the parasitic forms
That seem to keep her up but drag her down—
Will leave her space to burgeon out of all
Within her—let her make herself her own
To give or keep, to live and learn and *be*
All that harms not distinctive womanhood.[20]

Test your love by these ideals:
How do I love thee? Let me count the ways.
I love thee to the *depth and breadth and height*
My soul can reach, when feeling out of sight
For the ends of Being and Ideal grace.
I love thee *to the level of everyday's*
Most quiet need, by sun and candle-light.
I love thee freely, as men strive for right;
I love thee purely, as they turn from praise.
I love thee with the passion put to use
In my old griefs, and with my childhood's faith.
I love thee with a love I seemed to lose
With my lost saints,—I love thee with the breath,
Smiles, tears, of all my life!—and, if God choose,
I shall but love thee better after death.[21]

      The night has a thousand eyes,
        And the day but one;
      Yet the light of the bright world dies
        With the dying sun.

      The mind has a thousand eyes,
        And the heart but one;
      Yet the light of the whole life dies
        When love is done.[22]

Love is long:

True love is but a humble, lowborn thing, And hath its food served up in earthen ware; IT IS A THING TO WALK WITH, HAND IN HAND, THROUGH THE EVERY DAYNESS OF THIS WORKDAY *world*, Baring its tender feet to every flint, Yet letting not one heart-beat go astray From Beauty's law of plainness and content; A simple, fireside thing, whose quiet smile Can warm earth's poorest hovel to a home; Which, when our autumn cometh, as it must. And life in the chill wind shivers bare and leafless, Shall still be blest with Indian-summer youth In bleak November, and, with thankful heart, Smile on its ample stores of garnered fruit, As full of sunshine to our aged eyes As when it nursed the blossoms of our spring.[23]

In the degree that we love will we be loved.[24]

Everyone has need of loving:
Folks need a lot of loving in the morning;
    The day is all before, with cares beset—
The care we know, and they that give no warning;
    For love is God's own antidote for fret.

Folks need a heap of loving at the noontime—
    In the battle full, the moment snatched from strife,
Halfway between the waking and the croontime,
    While bickering and worriment are rife.

Folks hunger so for loving at the night time,
    When wearily they take them home to rest—
At slumber song and turning-out-the-light time—
    Of all the time for loving that's the best.

Folks want a lot of loving every minute—
   The sympathy of others and their smile!
Till life's end, from the moment they begin it,
   Folks need a lot of loving all the while.[25]

I would not have this perfect love of ours
Grow from a single root, a single stem,
Bearing no goodly fruit, but only flowers
That idly hide life's iron diadem:
It should grow alway like that eastern tree
Whose limbs take root and spread forth constantly;
That love for one, from *which there doth not spring*
Wide love for all, is but *a worthless thing.*
Look inward through the depths of thine own soul.
How is it with thee? *Art thou sound* and whole?
Doth narrow search show thee no earthly stain?
BE NOBLE! AND THE NOBLENESS THAT LIES
IN OTHER MEN, SLEEPING, BUT NEVER DEAD,
WILL RISE IN MAJESTY TO MEET THINE OWN;
Then wilt thou see it gleam in many eyes.
Then will pure light around thy path be shed,
And thou wilt nevermore be sad and lone.[26]

Love is not a placid thing—

  If Love should count you worthy, and should deign
    One day to seek your door and be your guest,
    Pause! ere you draw the bolt and bid him rest,
  If in your old content you would remain.
  For *not alone he enters;* in his train
    Are angels of the mists, the onely quest,
    Dreams of the unfulfilled and unpossessed,
  And sorrow, and Life's immemorial pain.

He wakes desires you never may forget,
   He shows you stars you never saw before,
   He *makes you share* with him, for evermore,
The burden of *the world's divine regret.*
How wise you were to open not! and yet,
   How poor if you should turn him from the door.[27]

   Mary, since first I knew thee, to this hour,
   My love hath deepened, with my wiser sense
   Of what in Woman is to reverence;
   Thy clear heart, fresh as e'er was forest flower,
   Still opens more to me its beauteous dower;
   But let praise hush,—Love asks no evidence
   To prove itself well-placed: . . .
   This is enough, and we have done our part
   If we but keep it spotless as it came.[28]

   Music, when soft voices die,
   Vibrates in the memory—
   Odors, when sweet violets sicken,
   Live within the sense they quicken,
   Rose-leaves, when the rose is dead,
   Are heaped for the beloved's bed;
   And so thy thoughts, when thou art gone,
   Love itself shall slumber on.[29]

Love suffereth long, and is kind; love envieth not; love
vaunteth not itself, is not puffed up, doth not behave itself
unseemly, seeketh not her own, is not easily provoked,
thinketh no evil; rejoiceth not in iniquity, but rejoiceth in
the truth, beareth all things, believeth all things, hopeth all
things, endureth all things. Love never faileth.[30]

REFLECTION

The height of man's mental and spiritual emotions is Love,—love of parents for their children, love of children for their parents, and love of a man and woman which culminates in marriage, civilization's high sacrament.

True love is not an earth-born thing. It is a rarity, and bears the characteristics found in rare things. True love is kind. It does not alter when it alteration finds. True love is a love that gives and takes, never dying of its own accord. It can be killed only by the one it is bestowed upon. It can weather hardships, sorrows, and all earthly things so long as the rules of love are not broken.

Love—like friendship—is governed by the law of cause and effect. The rewards of love are as great as the efforts contributed to gain it. If love is built on a strong foundation of respect and admiration and grows little by little with tiny deeds of kindness cementing it firmly,—with consideration for the welfare of both individuals,—then, love will live forever, faithful and undying.

There is no place in true love for disrespect, criticism, selfishness or neglect. Occasionally, it is wise to ask ourselves, "Am I kind? Am I considerate? Am I selfish? Am I thinking of my own personal desires or am I thinking of the true welfare of all concerned? Do I respect the individuality of my loved one's interests, desires and opinions, or do I expect them to co-incide with my own?"

Like other rare things, love is destructible. Because love is an intangible thing, we do not always recognize the tangible attributes that control it. Because it is freely given, we often disregard its value. Love is most precious. It is fulfillment of the Law and deserves our knowledge and diligence to preserve it, guard it from tarnish, injury or destruction.

7 FAMILY LIFE

Family life contributes immensely to an individual's happiness. Only in a happy homelife can complete contentment be found.

We *find* our lives *in losing* them in the *service* of others."[1]

"I love you, Mother," said little Ben;
  Then, *forgetting his work*, his cap went on,
And he was off to the garden swing,
  And left her the water and wood to bring.

"I love you, Mother," said rosy Nell—
  "I love you better than tongue can tell";
Then she *teased and pouted* full half the day,
  'Till her mother rejoiced when she went to play.

"*I love you*, Mother," said little Fan;
  "*Today I'll help* you all I can;
How glad I am that school doesn't keep!"
  So she rocked the babe till it fell asleep.

Then, stepping softly, she fetched the broom,
  And swept the floor and tidied the room;
Busy and happy all day was she,
  Helpful and happy as child could be.

"I love you, Mother," again they said,
  Three little children going to bed;
How do you think that mother guessed
  Which of them really loved her best?[2]

Careless words are cruel:

If I had known in the morning
How wearily all the day
    The word, unkind,
    Would trouble my mind
I said when you went away,
I had been more careful, darling,
    Nor given you needless pain;
But we vex "our own"
With look and tone
    We might never take back again.

For though in the quiet evening
You may give me the kiss of peace,
    Yet *it might be*
    That never for me
The pain of the heart would cease.
How many go forth in the morning
    That never come home at night,
And *hearts have broken*
For *harsh words spoken*
    That sorrow *can ne'er set right.*

We have careful *thought for the* stranger,
And *smiles for* the sometime *guest,*
    But oft *for "our own"*
    The bitter tone,
Though we love "our own" the best.

Ah! lips with the curve impatient,
    Ah! brow with the look of scorn,
'Twere a cruel fate
Were the night too late
    To undo the work of the morn.[3]

Immortal words:

Mid pleasures and palaces though we may roam,
Be it ever so humble, there's no place like home;
A charm from the sky seems to hallow us there,
Which, seek through the world, is ne'er met with elsewhere.
    Home, home, sweet, sweet, home.
There's no place like home, oh, there's no place like home!

An exile from home, splendor dazzles in vain;
Oh, give me my lowly thatched cottage again!
The birds sing gayly, that came at my call—
Give me them—and the peace of mind, dearer than all!
    Home, home, sweet, sweet home!
There's no place like home, oh, there's no place like home!

I gaze on the moon as I tread the drear wild,
And feel that my mother now thinks of her child,
As she looks on that moon from our own cottage door
Thro' the woodbine, whose fragrance shall cheer me no
    more.
    Home, home, sweet, sweet home.
There's no place like home, oh, there's no place like home.

How sweet 'tis to sit 'neath a fond father's smile,
And the caress of a mother to soothe and beguile,
Let others delight mid new pleasures to roam,
But give me, oh, give me, the pleasure of home,
    Home, home, sweet, sweet home.

To thee I'll return, overburdened with care;
The heart's dearest solace will smile on me there;
No more from that cottage again will I roam;
Be it ever so humble, there's no place like home.
    Home, home, sweet, sweet home.
There's no place like home, oh, there's no place like home.[4]

REFLECTION

"Build your House Upon a Rock" was the advice of centuries ago. There is no stronger rock than true love.

Those who are wise build their homes—their marriage—on that rock of true love. The holy bonds of matrimony should be entered into soberly, sanely, and with knowledge of what to expect of marriage. For marriage is not a temporary thing, nor is it an individual thing. Marriage is not an end in itself. It is Life and has for its purpose, not the gratification of individual desire, but the highest good of civilization. It is an institution formed and sanctioned by society for the development of the highest type of progressive, contented citizenship.

Marriage is a vital part of Life and like any other partnership or business, it has its periods of depression and periods of elation. The same principles used in business can profitably be employed in marriage. Patience, willingness to sacrifice, and tolerance help to avoid friction.

When the monotony of household duties weighs us down, when we never get to the end of routine jobs, or of sickness, or of bills, it is well to remember as in other aggravations, "This too shall Pass Away." The household disorder caused by children is only for a short period in life. All too quickly it ceases. The aggravations and inconveniences of constant illness also pass away and are a part of life, not of marriage. The sleepless nights pass, and, all too soon, we have more time than we desire for sleep. The poor men and women have no monopoly on the cares and worries in life. Rich and poor share alike in all experiences.

We are struggling together to carry on in the maze of seemingly insolvable problems. Together, we are all searching for the secret formula that will give us the answer to the problems of humanity. All of us are striving with the same soul-hungering desire for happiness and peace. Separately, we will not find it. Together we can give it to the future citizens.

8 LIFE'S TRUE VALUES

The true values of life are not those that can be measured in dollars.

"For what doth it profit a man if he gains the whole world and lose his own soul?"[1]

Lay not up for yourselves *treasures upon earth,* where moth and dust doth corrupt and where thieves break through and steal. But *lay up* for yourselves *treasures in heaven,* where neither moth nor rust doth corrupt, and where thieves do not break through nor steal.[2]

> Woe to that land, to conquering ills a prey,
> Where wealth accumulates and men decay.[3]

It's good to have money and the things that money can buy. But it's good, too, to check up once in a while and MAKE SURE that YOU HAVEN'T LOST THE THINGS that money CAN'T buy.[4]

> True worth is in BEING, *not seeming,—*
> In *doing,* each day that goes by,
> *Some little good—not in dreaming*
> *Of great things to do by and by.*[5]

We are so busy with facts in this age, we have become somewhat *indifferent to Values*—art, literature, music, and the like. Material interests smother values.[6]

True worth is not found in glory or power:

The boast of heraldry, the pomp of power
   And all that beauty, all that wealth e'er gave,
Awaits alike the inevitable hour.
   The paths of glory lead but *to the grave.*

. . . .

Can storied urn or animated bust
   Back to its mansion call the fleeting breath?
Can Honor's voice provoke the silent dust,
   Or Flattery soothe the dull cold ear of Death?[7]

An ounce of prevention is worth a pound of cure.[8]

God reads the soul, and not the face;
   He hears the thoughts, and not the tongue,
In Heaven the features wear no grace
   Save that which round the spirit hung;
And only they are lovely seen
   Whose lives on earth have noble been.[9]

It isn't so much *what you do dear,*
As the things you leave undone
That leaves a bit of heartache
At the setting of the Sun.[10]

Victories that are easy are cheap. Those only are worth
having which come as the result of hard fighting.[11]

Our *character* is but the *stamp* on our souls *of the free*
choices of good and evil we have made through life.[12]

> *It is not* growing like a tree
> In *bulk, doth make man better be;*
> Or standing long an oak, three hundred year,
> To fall a log at last, dry, bald, and sear;
> A lily of the day
> Is fairer far in May;
> Although it fall and die that night,
> It was the plant and flower of light.
> In small proportions we just beauties see,
> And in short measures life may perfect be.[13]

Understand, however, that *every man is* WORTH *just so much as the things are worth about which he busies himself.* All things are implicated with one another, and the bond is holy; and there is hardly anything unconnected with any other thing. For things have been co-ordinated and they combine to form the same universe. For there is one universe made up of all things, and one God who provides all things, and one substance, and one law, one common reason in all intelligent animals, and one truth.[14]

Good reputation has value:

> *Good name* in man and woman, dear my lord,
> Is the immediate *jewel of their souls;*
> Who steals my purse steals trash; 'tis something,
> nothing;
> 'Twas mine, 'tis his, and has been slave to thousands;
> But he that filches from me my good name
> Robs me of that which enriches him not,
> And leaves me poor indeed.[15]

Think not so much of what thou hast not, as of what thou hast; but *of the things that thou hast, select the best,* and *then reflect how eagerly they would have been sought,*

if thou hadst them not. At the same time, however, take
care that thou dost not through being so pleased with them
accustom thyself to over-value them, so as to be disturbed
if ever thou shouldst not have them.[16]

Dante pictured the *emptiness* of aimless, *idle society* as
the *first step downward* in human nature.[17]

Are you just taking the froth off of life?
>   But *pleasures are like poppies* spread,
>   You *seize the flow'r, the bloom is shed*
>   Or like the snow falls in the river,
>   A moment white—*then melts forever*
>   Or like the borealis race,
>   That flit ere you can point their place;
>   Or like the rainbow's lovely form
>   Evanishing amid the storm.[18]

Not education, but character, is man's greatest need and
man's greatest safeguard.[19]

How can a man learn to know himself? In the measure
in which thou seekest to do thy duty shall thou know what
is in thee.

>   *But what is thy duty?*
>   *The demand of the hour.*[20]

They are slaves who dare not be in the right with two or
three.[21]

>   That man is rich;—
>   Who gives the world the best he has
>   From day to day;

Who sees the good in every class
On life's highway;
Who never tries his wealth to mass
But gives away;
Who never robs ANOTHER'S *heart*
Of any joy;
Who never tries good friends to part
Or to *destroy*
The *hope that's groping for a start*
In every boy;
Who finds a joy in birds and flowers
And babbling brooks;
Who loves the sunshine and the showers—
The shady nooks;
Whose soul within him never cowers
But upward looks;
Who values most the priceless things
Not bought with gold;
Whose voice with kindness ever rings
To young and old;
Who, with his sunshine, ever brings
A joy untold.[22]

Die when we may, I want it said of me, by those who knew me best, that I always *plucked a thistle* and *planted a flower*, when I thought a flower would grow.[23]

There is not a man or woman, however poor they may be, but have in their power, by the grace of God, *to leave behind* them the grandest thing on earth, *character*; and their children will rise up after them and thank God that their mother was a pious woman, or their father a pious man.[24]

What sunshine is to the flowers, smiles are to humanity. They are but trifles, to be sure; but, scattered along life's pathway, the good they do is inconceivable.[25]

> They talk about a woman's sphere.
>   As though it had a limit;
> There's not a place in earth or heaven
> There's not a task to mankind given,
> There's not a blessing or a woe,
> There's not a whisper, yes, or no,
> There's not a life, or death, or birth,
> That has a feather's weight of worth,
>   Without a woman in it.[26]

We need not be so concerned over how we die if we live honestly.[27]

Honesty has real worth:

> *A prince can make a belted knight,*
>   A marquis, duke, an' a' that;
> But *an honest man's aboon his might,*
>   Guid faith, he mauna fa that.
> For a' that, an' a' that,
>   Their dignities, an' a' that,
> The *pith o' sense an' pride o' worth,*
>   *Are higher rank* than a' that.
>
> Then let us pray that come it may,
>   (As come it will for a' that)
> That *sense and worth,* o'er a' the earth,
>   *Shall bear the gree,* an' a' that.

For a' that, an' a' that,
   It's coming yet, for a' that,
That man to man, the world o'er,
   Shall brithers be for a' that.[28]

A real home has true value:
Mid pleasures and palaces though we may roam,
Be it ever so humble, THERE'S NO PLACE LIKE HOME.
A charm from the skies seem to hallow us there,
Which, seek through the world is ne'er met with else-
   where.[29]

The things of every day are all *so sweet;*
   The morning meadows set with dew,
The dance of daisies in the moon, the blue
   Of far-off hills where twilight shadows lie,
The night with all its tender mystery of sound
   And silence, and God's starry sky.
Oh! life—the whole of life—is far too fleet,
   The things of every day are all so sweet.

The *common things of life* are *all so dear;*
   The waking in the warm half-gloom
To find again the old familiar room,
   The scents and sights and sounds that never tire,
The homely work, the plans, the lilt of baby's laugh,
   The crackle of the open fire;
The waiting, then the footsteps coming near,
   The opening door, the hand-clasp and the kiss—
Is Heaven not, after all, the Now and Here,
   The common things of life are all so dear?[30]

Self-sacrifice is the basis and essence of virtue, so those
virtues are the most meritorious that have cost the greatest
effort to attain.[31]

So the last shall be first, and the first last; for many may
be called, but few chosen.[32]

WHEN HE HAS MORE THAN HE CAN EAT
TO FEED A STRANGER'S NOT A FEAT.

When he has more than he can spend
It isn't hard to give or lend.

Who gives but what he'll never miss
Will never know what giving is.

He'll win few praises from his Lord
Who does but what he can afford.

THE WIDOW'S MITE TO HEAVEN WENT
BECAUSE REAL SACRIFICE it meant.[33]

Sweet are the thoughts that savor of content;
    The *quiet mind is richer than a crown;*
Sweet are the nights in careless slumber spent;
    The poor estate scorns fortune's angry frown;
Such sweet *content*, such minds, such *sleep*, such bliss,
    Beggars enjoy, when princes oft do miss.

The homely house that harbors quiet rest;
    The cottage that affords no pride nor care;
The mean that 'grees with country music best,
    The sweet consort of mirth and music's fare;
Obscured life sets down a type of bliss;
    A mind content both crown and kingdom is.[34]

MY MIND to me A KINGDOM IS,
    Such present joys therein I find
That it excels all other bliss

That earth affords or grows by kind;
Though much I want which most would have,
   Yet still my mind forbids to crave.

No princely pomp, no wealthy store,
   No force to win the victory,
No wily wit to salve a sore,
   No shape to feed a loving eye;
To none of these I yield as thrall:
   For why? My mind doth serve for all.

I see how plenty surfeits oft,
   And *hasty climbers* soon do *fall;*
I see that *those who are aloft*
   Mishap doth threaten most of all;
They *get with toil,* they *keep with fear:*
   Such cares my mind could never bear.

Content to live, this is my stay;
   I seek no more than may suffice;
I press to bear no haughty sway;
   Look, what I lack my mind supplies:
Lo, thus I triumph like a king,
   Content with that my mind doth bring.

Some have too much, yet still do crave;
   I little have, and seek no more.
They are but poor, though much they have,
   And I am rich with little store:
They poor, I rich; they beg, I give;
   They lack, I leave; they pine, *I live.*

I laugh, not at another's loss;
   I grudge not at another's pain;
No worldly waves my mind can toss;

My slate at one doth still remain:
I fear no foe, I fawn no friend;
I loathe not life, nor dread my end.[35]

Solitude is very sad,
Too much company is twice as bad.[36]

Things of lasting value—Truth:
Truth never dies. The ages come and go.
The mountains wear away, the stars retire.
Destruction lays earth's mighty cities low;
And empires, states and dynasties expire;
But caught and handed onward by the wise,
TRUTH NEVER DIES.

Though unreceived and scoffed at through the years;
Though made the butt of ridicule and jest;
Though held aloft for mockery and jeers,
Denied by those of transient power possessed,
Insulted by the insolence of lies,
Truth never dies.

It answers not. It does not take offense,
But with a mighty silence bides its time;
As some great cliff that braves the elements
And lifts through all the storms its head sublime,
It ever stands, uplifted by the wise;
And never dies.

As rests the Sphinx amid Egyptian sands;
As looms on high the snowy peak and crest,
As firm and patient as Gibraltar stands,
So truth, unwearied, waits the era blest
When men shall turn to it with great surprise.
Truth never dies.[37]

O health! *health!* the blessing of the rich, the riches of the poor, who can buy thee at too dear a rate, since there is no enjoying the world without thee?[38]

REFLECTION

The foregoing authors have given us insight into the real values in life. The real value of any incident, or any thing depends on viewpoint. Value does not depend on size. Material things have no true value. The things we do, do not offset the things we leave undone. It is not how much you do, but how well you do it that is important. Luxuries and pleasures do not make for real happiness. Often we find that "pleasures are like poppies spread, you seize the flow'r, the bloom is shed"—always "Evanishing" without much left behind. Seek the real and lasting pleasures of life. Sometimes we think happiness can be found in the pursuit of thrills, but only the things that are eternally and fundamentally right create and prolong the thrills;—those that are wrong limit and destroy the pleasures of living. Repetition of any stimulus finally ceases to give pleasure and boredom and positive pain occur.

The "don'ts" and "musts" of civilization which surround us from birth are not intended to restrict life, but to enlarge it. Life is to be lived, widely and deeply as possible. The greater values must always be put before the less important values, keeping proper proportion in life.

A good reputation; a clear conscience; appreciation of nature; a peaceful heart; the knowledge of having given happiness to others; a trained and well-filled mind; satisfaction from duty well done; faith in the outcome of right; contentment; well-adjusted social relationships; these make for true happiness.

9 HUMOR

Humor oils the wheels of life and helps to keep it running smoothly.

"One of the best things to have up your sleeve is a funny bone."[1]

Digging wells is about the only business where you don't have to begin at the bottom.

If you must carry a chip on your shoulder, get a job in a lumber yard, where it won't be noticed.

To get nowhere—follow the crowd.

Some of the "room at the top" is created by the men who go to sleep there and fall off.

Another need of the age is less scheming to get by without working and more working to get by without scheming.

Most people are color blind—they think they are blue when they are only *yellow.*

You can't retire on the money you waste.

After all is said and done, more is said than done.

Speech is like a wheel; the longer the spoke the greater the tire.

The best way to get rid of your duties is to discharge them.

Easy street is hard to find.

Any man who agrees with his wife can have his own way.

DO UNTO OTHERS AS THOUGH YOU WERE THE OTHERS.

Don't worry because the tide is going out—it always comes back.

CHEER UP! Birthdays are like measles—we all have them.

Nothing has put so many men on their feet as an alarm-clock.

Some women are foolish—but the Almighty had to make some matches for the men.

It would be shocking if some men preached what they practice.

Forgive and forget. The first helps your soul. The second, your liver.

Shun idleness,—it is the rust that attaches itself to the most brilliant metals.[1]

Some of your grief you have cured,
   And the sharpest you still have survived,
But what torments of grief you endured
   From evils which never arrived.[2]

You know the model of your car,
You know just what its powers are.
You treat it with a deal of care
Nor tax it more than it will bear.
But as for self—that's different;
Your mechanism may be bent,
Your carburetor gone to grass,
Your engine just a rusty mass.
Your wheels may wobble and your bogs
Be handed over to the dogs.
And you skip and skid and slide
Without a thought of things inside.
What fools indeed, we mortals are
To lavish care upon a car
With ne'er a bit of time to see
About our own machinery![3]

Jumping at conclusions is about the only mental exercise some people take.

Why does nature give the big voice to the little thinker?

A green man can make a success, but a blue man never can.

It is easier to live within than without one's income.

It takes thirty-four muscles to frown, and only thirteen to smile. *Why* make *the extra effort?*

A woman's mind ought to be cleaner than a man's, she changes it so much oftener.

It is not true that dark-haired women marry first; it is quite as often the light-headed ones.

More horse-sense and less horse-power would improve motor driving.

Some people practice economy only with the truth.

More headwork at crossings—less surgical work at hospitals.

If we lock up all our feeble-minded, who will write our popular songs?

Talk may be cheap, but not over long distance.

Some people's expenditure of speech is too great for their income of ideas.

What we need is an amendment compelling everybody over eighteen to work.

Nothing needs reforming like the other people's habits.

There is always a penalty for exceeding the feed-limit.

No matter what your lot in life may be, build something on it.

If the worst happens, and you get the best of it, it isn't so bad after all.

The real engagement stone is a diamond; but the marriage stone is, of course, a grindstone.

Have you ever noticed that the knocker is always on the outside of the door?

No speckled young apple ever had a ripe old age.

The tattler who tattles to you will tattle about you. Don't listen in.

Some of the footprints on the sands of time are pointed the wrong way.

Love at first sight is often cured by a second look.

The rest of your days depend upon the rest of your nights.

Running expenses keep father out of breath.

"Don't care" kills more people than care.

No rewards are offered for finding fault.

Running people down is a bad habit, whether you are a gossip or a motorist.

A good memory test; try to remember the things you worried about last week.

Everybody makes mistakes; that's why they put erasers on pencils.

Why are people so dissatisfied with everybody else so satisfied with themselves?

Hardship makes hardihood.

If you cannot make light of your troubles, keep them dark.

So live that you wouldn't be afraid to sell the family parrot to the town gossip.

The world, you advise me, is utterly wrong,
Your life, you assure me, is sad;
Whenever we meet you are there with a long
Sad tale of the trouble you've had.

Your rent had been raised and you think it's unfair;
Your wife is a terrible scold;
You are losing your money, your mind and your hair;
You are getting (you feel it) a cold.

That luck is against you, my friend, I can see,
You have reason, I grant, to be blue,
BUT WHY MUST YOU TELL ALL YOUR TROUBLES TO ME,
WHEN I'M DYING TO TELL MINE TO YOU?[4]

"Men will talk about little things and great things, *as if they knew* which were little and which were great."[1]

THINK NAUGHT A TRIFLE, THOUGH IT SMALL APPEARS;
SMALL SANDS MAKE MOUNTAINS, MOMENTS MAKE THE YEAR,
AND TRIFLES, LIFE![2]

> *Nothing useless is, or low;*
>   Each thing *in its place* is best;
> And what seems but idle show
>   Strengthens and supports the rest.[3]

What dire offence from *amorous causes* springs,
What mighty contests rise *from trivial* things.[4]

For want of *a* nail the shoe was lost,
For want of *a* shoe the horse was lost;
For want of *a* horse the rider was lost, and all.
For want of *a* horseshoe nail.[5]

Many estates *are spent* in the getting, since women for teas forsook spinning and knitting, and men for punch forsook hewing and splitting.[6]

Diligence and moderation are the best steps whereby to climb to any excellency. Nay, it is rare if there be any other way. The heavens send not down their *rain* in floods, but *by drops*, and tiny distillations. A man is neither good nor wise, nor rich at once; yet softly creeping up these hills, he shall every day better his prospects; till at last he gain the top.[7]

> Heaven is not reached *at a single bound,*
> We build the ladder by which we rise
> From the lowly earth to the vaulted skies,
> And we mount to its summit *round by round.*[8]

He that is *faithful in* that which is *least,* is faithful also *in much;* and he that is *unjust in* the *least,* is unjust also in much.[9]

And whosoever shall *give* to drink unto one of these *little ones* a cup of cold water, verily I say unto you, he shall in no wise lose his reward.[10]

Each day is like a furrow lying before us; our *thoughts, desires,* and *actions are the seed* that *each minute* we drop into it, without seeming to perceive it. The furrow finished, we commence upon another, then another, and again another; *each day* presents a fresh one, and so on to the end of life . . . sowing, ever sowing. And all we have *sown springs up, grows,* and *bears fruit,* almost unknown to us. . . . Is there not a thought in this that should make us reflect?[11]

> *Loving words* will *cost* but *little,*
> Journeying up the hill of life;
> But they make the weak and weary
> Stronger, braver, for the strife.

Do you count them only TRIFLES?
What to earth are sun and rain?
Never was a kind word wasted;
Never was one said in vain.[12]

Sow a seed, and you will reap a habit; sow a habit, and you will reap a character; sow a character, and you will reap a destiny.[13]

Great things never do really happen to anyone; that is, the great things always come in *shoals of countless little things,* which look like insignificant atoms as we pass through them, and only seem a shoal when we have passed beyond them.[14]

THERE IS NO GREAT AND NO SMALL TO THE SOUL THAT MAKETH ALL.[15]

In the least things have faith, yet distrust in the greatest of all.[16]

Do not despond because your means of doing good appear trifling and insignificant, for though one soweth and another reapeth, yet *it is God who giveth the increase.*[17]

Words are mighty, words are living;
Serpents with their venomous stings,
Or bright angels crowding round us
With heaven's light upon their wings.
Every word has its own spirit,
True or false, that *never dies;*
Every word man's lips have uttered
Echoes in God's skies.[18]

How far that little candle throws his beams.
So shines a good deed in a naughty world.

Heaven doth with us as we with torches do;
Not light them for themselves; for if our virtues
Did not go forth of us, 'twere all alike
As if we had them not.[19]

One by *one* thy duties wait thee;
   Let thy whole strength go to each,
Let no future dreams elate thee,
   Learn thou *first what these can teach.*[20]

One step at a time, and that well placed,
  We reach the grandest height;
One stroke at a time, earth's hidden stores
  Will slowly come to light;
One seed at a time, and the forest grows;
One drop at a time, and the river flows
  Into the boundless sea.

One word at a time, and the *greatest book*
  Is written and *is read;*
One stone at a time, and a palace rears
  Aloft its stately head;
One blow at a time, and the tree's cleft through,
And a city will stand where the forest grew
  A few short years before.

One foe at a time, and he subdued,
  And the conflict will be won;
One grain at a time, and the sands of life
  Will slowly all be run;

One minute, another, the *hours* thus fly;
One day at a time, and our lives speed by
   Into *eternity.*

One grain of knowledge, and that well stored,
   Another and more on them;
As time rolls on your mind will shine
   With many a garnered gem
Of thought and *wisdom.* And time will tell
"One thing at a time, and that done well,"
   Is wisdom's proven rule.[21]

     Daily, with souls that cringe and plot,
     We Sinais climb and know it not.[22]

Nothing comes by chance, for, in all the wide universe, *there is absolutely no such thing as chance. We bring what-ever comes.* Are we not satisfied with effects, the results? The thing then to do is to change the causes.[23]

   The Mountain and the Squirrel
   Had a quarrel,
   And the former called the latter "Little Prig."
   Bun replied:
   "You are doubtless very big;
   But all sorts of things and weather
   Must be taken in together
   To make up a year,
   And a sphere;
   And I think it no disgrace
   To occupy my place.
   If I'm not so large as you,
   You're not so small as I,
   And not half so spry;

I'll not deny you make
A very pretty squirrel track.
Talents differ; all is well and wisely put;
If I cannot carry forests on my back,
Neither can you crack a nut."[24]

Even a smile can grow and accomplish much:
    My father smiled this morning when
        He came downstairs, you see,
    At mother; and, when he smiled, then
        She turned and smiled at me;
    And when she smiled at me I went
        And smiled at Mary Ann
    Out in the kitchen; and she lent
        It to the baker's man.

    So then he smiled at someone whom
        He saw when going by,
    Who also smiled, and, ere he knew,
        Had twinkles in his eye;
    So he went to his office then,
        And smiled right at his clerk,
    Who put some more ink on his pen,
        And smiled back from his work.

    And when his clerk went home he smiled
        Right at his wife; and she
    Smiled over at his little child,
        As happy as could be;
    And then the little girlie took
        The smile to school; and, when
    She smiled at teacher from her book,
        Teacher smiled back again.

And then the teacher passed on one
   To little Jim McBride,
Who couldn't get his lessons done
   No matter how he tried;
And Jimmy took it home, and told
   How teacher smiled at him
When he was tired, and didn't scold,
   But said, "Don't worry, Jim."

And when I happened to be there
   That very night to play,
Jim's mother had a smile to spare,
   Which came across my way;
And then *I took it* for awhile
   Back home, and mother said;
"Here is *that very selfsame smile*
   Come back with us to bed."[25]

Tiny, seemingly insignificant things have great influence:—

The *first backward step* is almost *imperceptible;* it was those *tiny flakes* of snow, seeming to melt as they touch the earth, but *falling one upon another,* that have *formed* the *immense mass* which seems ready to fall and *crush us.*

Ah! if I tried to trace back, to what first led to that act of sin; *the thought* that produced the *desire;* the *circumstance* that gave rise to the thought, I should find something almost impreceptible; perhaps *a word,* a *useless explanation,* sought out of mere curiosity; a *hasty look,* cast I knew not wherefore, and which conscience prompted me to check; a prayer neglected, because it wearied me; work left undone, while I indulged in some day-dream, that flitted before my fancy. . . .

A week later, the *same things occur,* but this time more

prolonged; the stifled voice of *conscience is hushed*. Alas, let us stop there; each can complete the sad story for himself, and it is easy to draw the practical conclusion.[26]

"*Little by little*," an *acorn* said,
As it slowly sank in its mossy bed;
"I am *slowly growing every day*,
Hidden deep in the earth away."
Little by little each day it grew;
Little by little it sipped the dew
Downward it sent out a thread-like root;
Up in the air sprung a tiny shoot
Day after day, and year after year,
Little by little the leaves appear;
And the slender branches spread far and wide,
Till *the mighty oak* is the forest's pride.

"Little by little," said the thoughtful boy,
"Moment by moment, I'll well employ,
Learning a little every day,
And not spending all my time in play,
And still this rule in my mind shall dwell—
Whatever I do I'll do it well.
Little by little, I'll learn to know
The treasured wisdom of long ago;
And one of these days perhaps I'll see
That the world will be the better for me."[27]

"Drop a *stone* into the water—
In a moment it is gone,
But there are *a hundred ripples*
Circling on and on and on,

Say an *unkind word* this moment—
In a moment it is gone
But there are a *hundred ripples*
Circling on and on and on,
Say a *word of cheer* and splendor—
In a moment it is gone
But there are a *hundred ripples*
Circling on and on and on."[28]

REFLECTION

Little things oftentimes have greater value than big things. Someone said, "There are no little things." Could the cup of water exist without the drop of water? Can one say the minute is greater than the second? "Thou shalt not judge." No man knows which are the little things and which are the big. The things man terms as "little" sometimes influence a greater result than those things man terms as "big."

Matter is based on tiny units. Time has for its basic foundation the second. The spirit has for its foundation the dividing of a crust of bread, the administering of a cup of water, or the widow's mite. A kind word spoken in the time of need, a smile, the care of a little child, sometimes means more than great deeds. It is not for us to judge which actions are worth while and which do the most toward establishing the Kingdom in God's sight. "The first shall be the last, and the last shall be first."

"As every thread of gold is valuable, so is every moment of time."[1]

One of the greatest truths which is seldom realized is the sacredness of time. Every moment of time has its effect "plus or minus" on an individual's success both materially and spiritually.

If wishing could bring them back, If wishing could bring them back: The wrathful words that flew away To mar the joy of another's day; If wishing could bring them back.[2]

Time is capital. Invest it wisely.[3]

Lost: Somewhere between sunrise and sunset, two golden hours, each set with sixty diamond minutes. No reward is offered, for they are gone forever.[4]

A false balance is abomination to the Lord but a just weight is his delight.[5]

> We are but minutes, *little things,*
> Each one furnished with sixty wings
> With which we fly on our unseen track
> And *not a one of us ever comes back.*

We are but minutes, use us well,
For how we are used we must someday tell;
Who uses minutes has hours to use,
Who loses minutes—whole years must lose.[6]

There is a tide in the affairs of men,
Which taken at the flood, leads on to fortune;
  Omitted, all the voyage of their life
Is bound in shallows and in miseries;
  And we must take the current when it serve,
  Or lose our ventures.[7]

The Moving Finger writes; and having writ,
Moves on; nor all your Piety nor wit
Shall lure it back to cancel half a line.
Nor all your tears wash out a word of it![8]

       Tomorrow's a myth—
       Get busy forthwith!
       Today is a fact—
       Act, man act!

For *today is Life*, the very Life of Life, in its brief course lie all the varieties and realities of your existence, the bliss of growth, the story of action, the splendor of beauty.

For *yesterday is* already *a dream*, and *tomorrow* is only a *vision;*

But *today well lived* makes every yesterday a dream of happiness, And every *tomorrow's vision a hope*. Look well, therefore, to this Day. Such is the Salutation of the Dawn.[9]

Listen to the water mill, through the live-long day, how the clanking of its wheels wears the hours away. Languidly the autumn wind stirs the greenwood leaves; From the field the reapers sing, binding up the sheaves; And a proverb haunts my mind, as a spell is cast; *"The mill will never grind With the water that has passed."*

Take a lesson to thyself, Loving heart and true; Golden years are fleeting by, youth is passing, too; Learn to make the most of life, lose no happy day; Time will never bring thee back chances swept away. Leave no tender word unsaid, love while life shall last—"The mill will never grind with water that has passed."

Work while the daylight shines, man of strength and will, Never does the streamlet glide useless by the mill. *Wait not till tomorrow's* sun beams upon the way; *All thou canst call thine own lies in thy today. Power, intellect* and *health* may not, *cannot last;* "The mill will never grind with water that has passed."

Oh, the wasted hours of life That have drifted by, *Oh, the good we might have done,* lost without a sigh; *Love that we might once have saved by a single word,* Thoughts conceived but never penned, perishing unheard. Take a proverb to thine heart; take, oh, hold it fast—"The mill will never grind with water that has passed."[10]

Moments:—

> Like the dew on the mountain,
>   Like the foam on the river,
> Like the bubble on the fountain,
>   *Thou are gone, and forever.*[11]

The minutes have their trusts as they go by.[12]

> Time is
> Too slow for those who wait,
> Too swift for those who Fear,
> Too long for those who Grieve,

Too short for those who Rejoice;
But for those who Love,
Time is
Eternity.[13]

If you have hard work to do
Do it now.
Today the skies are clear and blue,
Tomorrow clouds may come in view,
Yesterday is not for you;
Do it now.[14]

Lost the day loitering, 'twill be the same story
To-morrow, and the next more dilatory,
For indecision brings its own delays,
And days are lost lamenting o'er lost days.
Are you in earnest? *Seize this very minute!*
What you can do, or think you can, *begin it!*
Only engage, and then the mind grows heated;
Begin it, and work will be completed.[15]

It's fine to have a blow-out in a fancy restaurant,
With terrapin and canvas back and all the wine you want;
To enjoy the flowers and music, watch the pretty women
    pass,
Smoke a choice cigar, and sip the wealthy water in your
    glass.
It's bully in a high toned joint to *eat and drink your fill,*
But it's quite another matter when you, *Pay the bill.*

It's great fun to go out every night on fun or pleasure bent;
To wear your glad rags always and to never save a cent;
To drift along regardless, have a good time every trip;

To hit the high spots sometimes and to let your chances
    slip;
To know you're acting foolish, yet to go on fooling still,
Till nature calls a show-down, and you Pay the bill.

Time has got a little *bill,* get wise while yet you may,
For the debit side's increasing in a most alarming way;
The things you had no right to do, the things you should
    have done,
They're all set down; it's up to you to pay for everyone
So eat, drink and be merry, have a good time if you will,
But God help you when the time comes and you Pay the
    bill.[16]

> Little drops of water,
>   Little grains of sand,
> Make a mighty ocean,
>   And the pleasant land.
>
> Thus the *little minutes,*
>   Humble though they be,
> *Make the mighty ages*
>   *Of eternity.*[17]

One more solemn thought; How old are you? Nineteen.
Have you reckoned the number of minutes that have elapsed
since your birth? The number is startling: nine millions,
three hundred and thirty-three thousand, two hundred. . . .
Each of those minutes has flown to God; *God has examined
them,* and *weighed them, and for them you must give account.*[18]

There is no such thing as "time" in eternity. Time is merely
the structure used to hold thoughts and actions together in

this world. When thoughts and actions cease and the change which we call death takes place, it does not mean that the soul departs from *Time*, (for the soul is still in the same place as it was and it will always remain where it was, unchangeable, and in the state of consciousness which it reached), but that *Time departs* from the soul, and Time continues only in the material thoughts and actions of those living.[19]

Work for the night is coming;
  Work through the morning hours;
Work while the dew is sparkling;
  Work 'mid springing flowers;
Work while the day grows brighter,
  Under the glowing sun;
Work, for the night is coming,
  When man's work is done.
Work, for the night is coming;
  Work through the sunny noon;
Fill brightest hours with labor,
  Rest comes sure and soon;
Give every flying minute
  Something to keep in store;
Work, for the night is coming,
  When man works no more.

Work, for the night is coming;
  Under the sunset skies,
While their bright tints are glowing,
  Work, for the daylight flies;
Work till the last beam fadeth,
  Fadeth to shine no more;
Work while the night is darkening.
  When man's work is o'er.[20]

REFLECTION

Time used and time unused both have results. Used min-
utes will some day be added up and will show their positive
results just as unused minutes will show their negative re-
sults. This rule of time applies to material results as well as
to spiritual outcomes. Each thought takes a second—oc-
cupies a definite amount of time. The sum of these thoughts
added make your life; therefore, one's thoughts strongly
affect his future—his success or his defeat. Every second
of one's time is making its impression on the universe.
Some day the test will come. One sees the sum total added
up to accomplish or fail in a purpose he desires and his own
used and unused seconds fight for him or against him. He
has wrought his own victory or his defeat.

A mans' material success in the world clearly shows he
has applied his mind and his time using the right laws and
that he worked in harmony with the laws for success. The
unsuccessful man has not applied the right laws and has
wasted much time. Time is irretrievable. It goes on and on,
waiting for no man, and its influence is tremendous. The
seconds tick by, habits are formed unconsciously as one
second piles upon another—little things—but they have
their strength in numbers and, as the tiny grains of sand
unite and form the shore that holds in check a mighty
ocean; these little things hold in check the ocean of life. The
impressions our daily habits make become stronger and
stronger, unrealized by us until the time suddenly arises
for the test. "Habit is a cable, we weave a thread of it each
day until it becomes so strong we cannot break it."

There comes a time when we need the help of every
strong habit we have formed. It is then that we "reap what
we have sowed" to the fullest degree. Lost time can never

be replaced. It is too late for any new agreements with one's soul. We must pay the price when it is demanded from our reserve funds.

When the test comes it may be a physical one. If the laws of hygiene and health have been disregarded, the price will be shattering at a time when the body is bankrupt of strength to pay it. The price must be paid, for health cannot be acquired in a moment when the crisis arises.

The test may come in sorrow, discouragement, or suffering that demands the strength of a great faith and a belief in the Power of Right.

It may be that the test will come in the material work-a-day world, where one's mentality will have to battle brilliant minds. If the mind has been carefully trained in good habits of thinking quickly and clearly, if it has been filled with the right information, it will be prepared. Canon Liddon says, "What we do on some great occasion will probably depend on what we already are, and what we are will be the result of previous years of self-discipline." Every second, every thought, every word, every action, every bit of knowledge picked up on life's way—even though entirely forgotten—unites—the positive with the affirmative side, the negative with the other side. We willfully make our own Heaven or Hell through preparedness or through indifference.

"It is the greatest of all mistakes to do nothing because you can only do little—*Do what you can.*"[1]

Do not criticize your part in the play of life; but *study it*, *understand it*, and then *play it*, sick or well, rich or poor, *with courage*, and with proper grace.[2]

DO NOT PRAY FOR EASY LIVES. PRAY TO BE STRONGER MEN. DO NOT PRAY FOR TASKS EQUAL TO YOUR POWERS. PRAY FOR POWERS EQUAL TO YOUR TASKS! Then the doing of your work shall be no miracle, but you shall be a miracle. Every day you will wonder at yourself, at the richness of life that has come to you by the Grace of God.[3]

Are *you* pleasant to live with? Keep this personal question before you, even if you are cocksure that you can answer, yes.[4]

Character is built out of circumstances—from exactly *the same materials* one man builds palaces, while another builds hovels.[5]

> *I have to live with myself,* and so
> *I want* to be for myself to know,
> *Always to look myself straight in the eye,*
> I don't want to stand, with the setting sun

And hate myself for the things I've done,
I want to go out with my head erect;
I want to deserve all men's respect;
But here in the struggle for fame and self
I want to be able to like myself.
I don't want to look at myself and know
That I'm bluster and bluff and empty show
I never can fool myself, and so
Whatever happens I want to be
Self-respecting and conscience free.[6]

It doesn't do to do much talking
   When you're mad enough to choke
For *the word that hits the hardest*
   Is the one that's never spoke.
Let the other fellow do the talking
   Till the storm has rolled away,
Then he'll do a heap of thinking
   'Bout *the things you didn't say.*[7]

The world is a looking-glass, and gives back to every man
the reflection of his own face. Frown at it, and it in turn
will look sourly upon you; laugh at it and with it, and it is
a jolly, kind companion.[8]

What thou wilt, Thou must rather enforce it with thy
smile, Than hew to it with thy sword.[9]

A lucky fellow you say—No, his luck is determined by
a good mother, a good constitution, habit of work, indomitable energy, determination which knows no defeat, un-
wavering decision, concentration, courage, self-mastery,
ability to say "no" and stick to it, strict integrity, honesty,

cheerful disposition, enthusiasm, high aim, and a noble purpose.[10]

Tact clinches the bargain, sails out of the bay, gets the votes in the Senate, spite of Webster and Clay.[11]

If you have built castles in the air, your work need not be lost; that is where they should be; now put foundations under them.[12]

When thou hast been compelled by circumstances to be disturbed in a manner, quickly return to thyself and do not continue out of tune longer than compulsion lasts; for thou wilt have more mastery over the harmony by continually recurring to it.[13]

> Be good sweet maid,
> Let whoe'r will be clever,
> *Do* noble deeds, *not dream them* all day long
> And so make life, death, and the vast forever
> One grand sweet song.[14]

A man cannot rightly or justly say—"This is my life, I can live it as I please," for he is responsible to God, first of all; to his family second; to his community third; and then to himself. He can do only that which has no direct or indirect ill effect on any of those to whom he is responsible.

Whatever you are by nature, keep to it; never desert your line of talent. Be what nature intended you for, and you will succeed; be anything else, and you will be ten thousand times worse than nothing.[15]

The greatest virtue is conservation, and the greatest folly is dissipation.[16]

The road to distinction must be paved with years of self denial and hard work.[17]

The first and best victory is to conquer self; to be conquered by self is of all things, the most shameful and vile.[18]

Govern thyself, and you will be able to govern the world.[19]

> For age and want, save while you may;
> No morning sun lasts a whole day.[20]

> Great estates may venture more,
> But little boats should keep near shore.[21]

If at first you don't succeed, Try, try again![22]

> Early to bed and early to rise
> Makes a man healthy, wealthy, and wise.[23]

> Then plow deep while sluggards sleep,
> And you shall have corn to sell and to keep.[24]

> Save and you will know,
> Dimes to dollars grow.[25]

And if once will not suffice, do it thrice![26]

The first hour in the morning is the rudder of the day.[27]

The longer I live, the more deeply am I convinced that that which makes *the difference between one man and another*—between the weak and the powerful, the great and insignificant, *is energy*—invincible determination—a purpose once formed, and then death or victory.[28]

How fortunate is he who, in this busy world, enjoys both the willingness and ability to help his fellow man.[29]

> Live for something, have a purpose
>   And that purpose keep in view;
> Drifting like a helmless vessel,
>   Thou cans't ne'er to life be true.[30]

Next to knowing when to seize an opportunity, the most important thing in life is to know *when to forego an advantage.*[31]

> If you can dress to make yourself attractive,
>   Yet not make puffs and curls your chief delight;
> If you can swim and row, be strong and active,
>   But of the gentler graces not lose sight;
> If you can dance without a craze for dancing,
>   Play without giving play too strong a hold;
> Enjoy the love of friends without romancing;
>   Care for the weak, the friendless and the old.

> If you can master French and Greek and Latin,
>   And not acquire, as well, a priggish mien;
> If you can feel the touch of silk and satin,
>   Without despising calico and jean;
> If you can ply a saw and use a hammer,
>   Can do a man's work when the need occurs;

Can sing when asked, without excuse or stammer,
  Can rise above unfriendly snubs and slurs.

If you can make good bread as well as fudges,
  Can sew with skill and have an eye for dust;
If you can be a friend and hold no grudges,
  A girl whom all will love, because they must.

If some time you should meet and love another,
  And make a home with faith and peace enshrined,
And you, its soul, a loyal wife and mother,
  You'll work out pretty nearly to my mind
The plan that's been developed through the ages,
  And win the best that life can have in store,
You'll be, my girl, a model for the sages—
  A woman whom the world will bow before.[32]

> That which before us lies in daily life,
>   Is the prime wisdom.[33]

How can it be known you are in earnest, *if the act follows not* upon the word?[34]

> *The best reward* of a kindly deed
>   *Is the knowledge* of having done it.[35]

For every effect there is a *perfect cause*—good luck is only another name for tenacity of purpose.[36]

There's a family nobody likes to meet,
They live, it is said, on Complaining Street,
In the city of Never-Are-Satisfied,
The river of Discontent beside.
They growl at that and they growl at this,

Whatever comes there is something amiss;
And whether their station be high or humble,
They are known by the name of Grumble.

The weather is always too hot or too cold,
Summer and winter alike they scold;
Nothing goes right with the folks you meet
Down on the gloomy Complaining Street.
They growl at the rain and they growl at the sun,
In fact, their growling is never done.
And *if everything pleased them*, there isn't a doubt
They'd growl that they'd nothing to grumble about.

And the worst thing is that *if any one stays*
Among them too long *he will learn their ways,*
And before he dreams of the terrible jumble
He's adopted into the family of Grumble.
So it were *wisest to keep our feet*
From wandering into Complaining Street;
And never to growl, whatever you do,
Lest we be mistaken for Grumblers too.[37]

The man who is there with the wallop and punch
  The one who *is* trained to the minute,
May well be around when the trouble begins,
  But you seldom will find he is in it;
For they let him alone when they know he is there
  For any set part in the ramble,
  To pick out the one who is shrinking and soft
  And not quite attuned to the scramble.

The one who is fixed for whatever they start
  Is rarely expected to prove it;
They pass him along for the next shot in sight
  Where they take a full wind-up and groove it;

For who wants to pick on a bull-dog or such
  Where a quivering poodle is handy,
When he knows he can win with a kick or a brick
  With no further trouble to bandy?[38]

Once I heard a saying
And I wish you knew it too
'Twas-never trouble trouble 'till
Trouble troubles you.[39]

Don't put off until tomorrow what you can do today—tomorrows never come.[40]

Don't sit around and talk about what you are going to do —Do it!

What seems luck to most people is only good judgment and promptness in seizing opportunities—trusting to chance —taking no chances—dominant persistence.[41]

Rogues do their work at night. Honest men work by day. It's all a matter of habit, and good habits in America make any man rich. Wealth is largely a result of habit.[42]

Think before you act. Think twice before you speak.[43]

Every day should be passed as if it were to be our last.[44]

He who overcomes others is strong—he who overcomes himself is far more powerful.[45]

There's a time for work and a time for play,
A time for everything good each day,
But *never a time* in this short life,
For quarrels and angry words and strife.[46]

The heart too often hath quailed with dread,
  And quite its courage lost,
By casting its glance *too far ahead*
  For the bridge *that never was crossed.*[47]

What we call luck is simply pluck,
  And the doing things over and over;
Courage and will, perseverance and skill,
  Are the four leaves of Luck's clover.[48]

There shall never be one lost good.
All we have willed or hoped or dreamed of
    good shall exist;
Not its semblance but itself.[49]

Do not pay too much attention to the stupid old body. *When you have trained it, made it healthy, beautiful,* and *your willing servant, why, then do not reverse the order* and *become its slave* and attendant. (The dog must follow the master, not the master the dog.)

Remember that if you walk away from it and leave it behind, it will have to follow you—it will grow by following, by continually reaching up to you. Incredibly beautiful it will become, and suffused by a kind of intelligence.

But if you turn and wait upon it—and its mouth and its belly and its sex-wants and all its little ape-tricks—preparing and dishing up pleasures and satisfactions for these. *Why, then, instead of the body becoming like you, you will become like the body,* incredibly stupid and unformed—going back in the path of evolution—you too with fish-mouth and toad belly, and *imprisoned in your own members,* as it were an Ariel in a blundering Caliban.

Therefore quite lightly and decisively at each turning-point in the path *leave your body a little behind*—

With its hungers and sleeps, and funny little needs and
vanities—Pay no attention to them:
Slipping out at last *a few steps in advance,* till it catch
you up again,
*Absolutely determined not to be finally bound and
weighted down by it,*
Or fossilized into one set form—
Which alone after all is death.[50]

Man, like a generous *vine,* supported lives;
The *strength he gains is from the embrace he gives.*[51]

Who may not strive may yet fulfil
The harder task of standing still.[52]

Oh, that mine eyes might closed be
To what concerns not me to see;
That deafness might possess my ear
To what concerns not me to hear.[53]

Be wiser than other people if you can, but do not tell
them so.[54]

Forget it. Drop the subject when you cannot agree; there
is no need to be bitter because you know you are right.[55]

You can easily determine the caliber of a man by ascer-
taining the amount of opposition it takes to discourage
him.[56]

"Let me do the thing that ought to be done, when it ought
to be done, as it ought to be done, whether I like to do it or
not.[57]

Would any man be *strong*, let him *work*; or *wise*, let him *observe* and *think*; or *happy*, let him *help*; or *influential*, let him *sacrifice* and *serve*.[58]

Suppose that men curse thee, or kill thee. . . . If a man stand by a pure spring and curse it, the spring does not cease to send up wholesome water.[59]

"There is dew in one flower and not in another," said Beecher, "*because one opens its cup and takes it in,* while the other closes itself and drops run off." Are you dissatisfied with today's success? It is the harvest of yesterday's sowing. Do you dream of a golden tomorrow? *We get* out of life just *what we put in it. The world has for us* just *what we have for it. It is a mirror* which reflects the faces we make. If we smile and are glad, it reflects a cheerful sunny face. If we are sour, irritable, mean, and contemptible, it still shows us the true copy of ourselves. The world is a whispering gallery which returns the echo of our voices. *What we say of others is said of us.* We shall find nothing in the world we do not find first in ourselves.[60]

It rests with the workman whether a rude piece of marble shall be squared into a horse-block, or carved into an Apollo, Psyche, or a Venus de Milo. It is yours if you choose to develop a spiritual form more beautiful than any of these, instinct with immortal life, refulgent with all the glory of character.[61]

About the middle of the 18th century, a light-house called Dunstan Pillar was built on Lincoln Heath to guide travelers over a trackless, barren waste, a veritable desert, almost in the heart of England.

But now it stands in the midst of a fertile region. No bar-

To him that overcometh a crown of life shall be; he with
the King of Glory Shall reign eternally.[3]

Years should teach wisdom, but There is a spirit in man:
and the inspiration of the Almighty giveth them understanding. Great men are not *always* wise, neither do the
ages understand judgment.[4]

Be ever watchful of your desires:
Our heart's desires are our perpetual prayers—not head
prayers, but heart prayers—and nature grants them.[5]

> I slept and dreamed that life was beauty;
> I woke and found that life was *duty*.[6]

I believe in Eternal Progression; I believe in a God, a
beauty and perfection to which I am to strive all my life
for assimilation.[7]

Cheerfulness is the offshoot of goodness.[8]

Certain thoughts are prayers. There are moments when
whatever be the attitude of the body, the soul is on its
knees.[9]

Only what we have wrought into our character during
life can we take away with us.[10]

> Roll on, thou deep and dark blue ocean—roll!
> Ten thousand fleets sweep over thee in vain;
> *Man* marks the earth with ruin—*his control*
> *Stops with the shore.*[11]

A charge to keep I have, A God to glorify; A never-
dying soul to save, And fit it for the sky.[12]

Always finish:—

> If a task is once begun,
> Never leave it 'till it's done.
> Be the labor great or small,
> Do it well or not at all.[66]

> If you your lips would keep from slips,
>   Five things observe with care;
> *Of whom you speak, to whom you speak,*
>   And *how* and *when* and *where.*

> If you your ears would save from jeers,
>   These things keep meekly hid;
> Myself and I, and mine and my,
>   And how I do and did.[67]

Oft fire is without smoke, and peril without show.[68]

> So live that when thy summons comes to join
> The innumerable caravan that moves
> To that mysterious realm, where each shall take
> His chamber in the silent halls of death,
> Thou go not, like the quarry-slave at night,
> Scourged to his dungeon, but, sustained and soothed
> By an unfaltering trust, approach thy grave
> Like one who wraps the drapery of his couch
> About him, and lies down to pleasant dreams.[69]

Their words are no slander whose words are all slander.[70]

Melancholy—the worst natural parasite—whosoever feeds him shall never be rid of his company.[71]

It is wisely written—
What is impossible to change
Is best to forget.[72]

"The boneless tongue, so small and weak,
Can crush and kill," declared the Greek.

"The tongue destroys a greater horde,"
The Turk asserts, "than does the sword."

A Persian proverb wisely saith,
"A lengthy tongue—an early death."

Or sometimes takes this form instead,
"Don't let your tongue cut off your head."

"The tongue can speak a word whose speed,"
Says the Chinese, "outstrips the steed;"

While Arab sages this impart,
"The tongue's great storehouse is the heart."

From Hebrew with the maxim sprung,
"Though feet should slip, ne'er let the tongue."

The sacred writer crown the whole:
"Who keeps the tongue doth keep his soul."[73]

REFLECTION

A word from the wise—from those who have had experience in life—is far more valuable than many realize. If we are wise we will take it and make use of it, thus saving our-

selves much time and grief. *Govern your tongue; control your mind, your habits, and your desires; be persistent; be unafraid; have a purpose and stick to it; be cheerful,* so say the wise.

No one ever gets anything worthwhile by accident. Our hidden desires act as constant prayers and sooner or later those desires are answered in the form we have worked towards. Biographies of great men prove that LIFE IS WHAT YOU MAKE IT!

Because many of us do not understand the laws of gravity, radio, wireless, and other scientific discoveries, shall we refuse to accept them as truth? Because we have not seen the land at the North Pole, should we refuse to believe that there is such a place? It is given to each of us to know only a small part of the knowledge to be gained in the universe. Each makes his contribution to the whole of knowledge. Millions testify to knowing God and his power which is working through the universe. Is it intelligent of scorners to refute the testimony of the wisest men of the ages and thus deprive themselves of joy which can be theirs? If we open our eyes and ears and hearts to see and hear the great messages that are for us along our journey through life we will learn to know the kingdom. We can get in touch with the Infinite through true brotherhood for "All are but parts of one stupendous whole and he who loves his brother best gets nearer God than all the rest."

"All that is at all lasts ever, past recall, Earth changes, but thy soul and God stands sure."[1]

"Lord! how in darkness can I see aright?"
Child! all the universe I fill with light;
Be true within, and truth shall cleanse thy sight.[2]

To him that overcometh a crown of life shall be; he with the King of Glory Shall reign eternally.[3]

Years should teach wisdom, but There is a spirit in man: and the inspiration of the Almighty giveth them understanding. Great men are not *always* wise, neither do the ages understand judgment.[4]

Be ever watchful of your desires:
Our heart's desires are our perpetual prayers—not head prayers, but heart prayers—and nature grants them.[5]

>   I slept and dreamed that life was beauty;
>   I woke and found that life was *duty*.[6]

I believe in Eternal Progression; I believe in a God, a beauty and perfection to which I am to strive all my life for assimilation.[7]

Cheerfulness is the offshoot of goodness.[8]

Certain thoughts are prayers. There are moments when whatever be the attitude of the body, the soul is on its knees.[9]

Only what we have wrought into our character during life can we take away with us.[10]

>   Roll on, thou deep and dark blue ocean—roll!
>   Ten thousand fleets sweep over thee in rain;
>   *Man* marks the earth with ruin—*his control*
>   *Stops with the shore.*[11]

A charge to keep I have, A God to glorify; A never-dying soul to save, And fit it for the sky.[12]

Be what thou seemest; live thy creed; Hold up to earth the torch divine;

Be what thou prayest to be made; Let the great Master's steps be thine.[13]

> Speak to him, thou, for *He heareth*
> And *spirit to spirit can speak.*
> Closer is He than breathing, and nearer
> Than hands and feet.[14]

More things are wrought by prayer, than this world dreams of.[15]

All noblest things are religious—not temples and martyrdoms only, but the best books, pictures, poetry, statues, and music.[16]

He prayeth well, who loveth well Both man and bird and beast. *He prayeth* BEST *who loveth best All things* both *great* and *small,* For the dear God who loveth us, He made and loveth all.[17]

> I know not where His islands lift
> Their fronded palms in air;
> I only know I cannot drift
> Beyond His love and care.[18]

When the kingdom is once found, life then ceases to be a plodding, and becomes an exultation, an ecstasy, a joy.[19]

Consider the waterfowl:

> There is a Power whose care
> Teaches thy way along that pathless coast—
> The desert and illimitable air—
> Lone wandering, but not lost.

He who, from zone to zone,
Guides through the boundless sky *thy certain flight,*
In the long way that I must tread alone,
  Will lead my steps aright.[20]

This is a vital principle in Christian life; we can give out
to others only what God has given to us.[21]

Not to the swift, the race;
Not to the strong, the fight;
Not to the righteous, perfect grace;
Not to the wise, the light.

But *often faltering feet*
Come surest to the goal;
And they who walk in darkness meet
The sunrise of the soul.

A thousand times by night
The Syrian hosts have died;
A thousand times the vanquished right
Hath risen, glorified.

The truth the wise men sought
Was spoken by a child;
The alabaster box was brought
In trembling hands defiled.[22]

The new church will be founded on moral science. Poets,
artists, musicians and philosophers, will be its prophet teachers. The noblest literature of the world will be its Bible—
love and labor its holy sacraments.[23]

Pour forth all the color, charm, and happiness you have to your friends, to your home, to your daily society, to the poor and sorrowful, the joyous and the prosperous. *Charm the world by love.* Brighten darkened lives, soften the rude, make a sunshine of peace in stormy places, cover the faults and follies of men with flowers of love. *Love others,* and you will spread the delight of youth over all you meet, and in doing so you will live intensely; for *you will have within not only your own life but also the lives of all whom you bless by love. That is the best religion,* the life of Christ, the very life of God.

That is to be at one with Him whose gentle smile kindles the universe, whose love, moving in the spring, is the beauty that enchants our senses and heart, and inspires our soul.[24]

Every attempt to make others happy, every sin left behind, every temptation trampled under foot, every step forward in the cause of what is good, is a step nearer the cause of Christ.[25]

Immortal life is something *to be earned by slow self-conquest,* comradeship with pain and patient seeking after higher truths. *We cannot follow* out our *wayward wills,* and *feed* our *baser appetites,* and give loose *rein* to *foolish tempers* year on year and then cry, "Lord, forgive me; I believe!" *And straightway bathe in glory;* men must learn GOD'S SYSTEM IS TOO FINE A THING FOR THAT. *The spark divine dwells in our souls and we can fan it to a steady flame* of light, and shine on to eternity, *or else neglect it* till it glimmers down to *death* and leaves us but the darkness of the grave. Each conquered passion feeds the living flame, *Each well-borne sorrow is a step toward God; faith cannot rescue* and no blood redeem *a soul that will not reason* and resolve.[26]

Not by one portal or one path alone
God's holy messages to men are known.[27]

PRAYER IS THE SOUL'S SINCERE DESIRE, UTTERED OR UN-
EXPRESSED.[28]

*If one takes the sun with him he can find no shadows. As
soon as the sun turns on a shadow, the shadow-darkness disappears. The same is true of life; if one takes God with him,
who is the Spirit of Light, sorrows and troubles of life dis-
appear.*

Christ has no hands but *our hands*
    To do his work today;
He has no feet but *our feet*
    To lead men in His way;
He has no tongue but *our tongues*
    To tell men how he died;
He has no help but *our help*
    To bring them to his side.

We are the only Bible
    The careless world will read;
We are the sinner's gospel,
    We are the scoffer's creed;
We are the Lord's last message
    Given in deed and word—
What if the line is crooked?
    What if the type is blurred?

What if our hands are busy
    With other work than his?
What if our feet are walking
    Where sin's allurement is?

What if our tongues are speaking
  Of things his lips would spurn?
How can we hope to help him
  Unless from him we learn?[29]

God of the Granite and the Rose!
  Soul of the sparrow and the Bee!
The mighty tide of being flows
  Through countless channels, *Lord, from Thee.*
It leaps to life *in grass* and *flower,*
  Through every grade of being runs,
Till from creation's radiant tower
  Thy glory flames in stars and suns.

God of the Granite and the Rose!
  Soul of the Sparrow and the Bee!
The mighty tide of Being flows
  Through all Thy creatures back to Thee.
Thus round and round the circle runs,
  A mighty sea without a shore,
While men and women, stars and suns,
  Unite to praise Thee evermore.[30]

Miracles happen to-day as always, if ye have eyes ye shall see; if ye have ears ye shall hear. Everything is true to-day that was true two thousand years ago.

There is but one law—God's law—it works with perfect accuracy: Truth is truth and stands always.

Use all your hidden forces. *Do not miss*
The *purpose of this life,* and *do not wait*
For *circumstance to* mold or *change your fate.*
In your own self lies destiny. Let this
Vast truth *cast out* all fear, all prejudice,

All hesitation. Know that you are great,
Great with divinity. So *dominate*
Environment, and enter into bliss.—
Love largely and hate nothing. *Hold no aim*
That does not chord with universal good.
Hear what the voices of the silence say,
All joys are yours if you put forth your claim,
Once let the spiritual laws *be understood,*
Material things must answer and obey.[31]

BE SINCERE IN ALL THINGS.

Jesus saith unto him, I am the way and the Truth, and
the life; no man cometh unto the Father, but by me.[32]

All true work is sacred; in all true work, were it but true
hand-labor, there *is something of divineness.* Labor, wide as
the Earth, has its summit in Heaven. Sweat of the brow;
and up from that to sweat of the brain, sweat of the heart;
which includes all Kepler calculations, Newton meditations,
all sciences, all spoken epics, all acted heroisms, martyrdoms
—up to that "Agony of bloody sweat," which all men have
called divine! Oh, brother! if this is not "worship," then, I
say, the more pity for worship; for this is the noblest thing
yet discovered under God's sky! Who art thou that complain-
est of thy life of toil? Complain not. . . .
Wondrous is the strength of cheerfulness.[33]

There are those who claim they are "unbelievers", but if
they would truly analyze their beliefs they would find they
believe as everyone believes in a higher Power. Do they not
plant seeds and wait to see them push above the ground be-
lieving they will grow? When it rains are they not confident

that soon the rain will stop according to a universal law al-
ways in operation? Do they not lie down at night content
to allow their senses to lock in sleep trusting a universal
Power will operate to unlock them in the morning? "There
is no unbelief: for thus by day and night unconsciously the
heart lives by that faith the lips deny."

God is a Spirit: and they that worship him must worship
him in spirit and in truth.[34]

> Build thee more stately mansions, O my soul,
>   As the swift seasons roll
>   Leave thou low-vaulted past
> Let each new temple, nobler than the last,
> Shut thee from heaven with a dome more vast,
>   *Till thou at length are free.*
> Leaving thy outgrown shell by life's unresting sea.[35]

O God, our Father, give me clean hands, and clean words
    and clean thoughts;
Help me to stand for the hard right against the easy wrong
Save me from habits that harm;
Teach me to work as hard and play as fair in Thy sight
Alone as if all the world saw
Forgive me when I am unkind and forgive others who are
    unkind to me;
Keep me ready to help others at some cost to myself
Send me chances to do a little good every day and to grow
    more like Christ.[36]

Jesus answered, "Verily, verily, I say unto thee, except a
man be born again, he cannot see the kingdom of God."[37]

Thy faith hath made thee whole.[38]

Great truths are portions of the soul of man;
Great souls are portions of Eternity;
Each drop of blood that e'er through true heart ran
With lofty message, ran for thee and me.[39]

God give us men! The time demands
Strong minds, great hearts, true faith and willing hands;
  Men whom the lust of office does not kill;
Men whom the spoils of office cannot buy;
  Men who possess opinions and a will;
Men who have honor; men who will not lie;
  Men who can stand before a demagogue
And scorn his treacherous flatteries without winking;
  Tall men, sun crowned, who live above the fog,
In public duty and *in private thinking.*
  For while the rabble with their thumb-worn creeds,
Their large professions and their little deeds
  Mingle in selfish strife; lo, Freedom weeps;
Wrong rules the land, and waiting justice sleeps.[40]

No servant can serve two masters; for either he will hate
the one and love the other; or else he will hold to the one,
and despise the other. Ye cannot serve God and mammon.[41]

*Some people plod through life doing their little jobs and
praying to their God in their little way. And as their view
expands into the bigness of the Universe they lose sight of
their God. Others living under the same circumstances do
their little jobs and pray to their God, but as the Universe
widens to their sight they see the gigantic marvels of it and
God in their growing mind becomes a new and greater God.*

The day's at the morn;
Morning's at seven;
The hillsides dew-pearled;

The lark's on the wing;
The snail's on the thorn;
God's in his Heaven—
All's right with the world.[42]

If through the joy or through the *sorrow* of life, *through*
love or the want of it, through the gaining of friends or the
loss of them, *we have been led to* dower our lives with the
friendship of God, we are possessed of the incorruptible, and
undefiled, and that passeth not away. The man *who has it*
has attained the secret *cheaply, though it had to be purchased*
with his heart's blood, with the loss of his dream of blessed-
ness.[43]

Pray to be perfect, though material leaven
Forbid the spirit so on earth to be;
But if for any wish thou darest not pray,
Then pray to God to cast that wish away.[44]

I live. This much I know; and I defy
The world to prove that I shall ever die!
But all men perish? Aye, and even so
Beneath the grasses lay this body low;
Forever close these eyes and still this breath;
All this, yet *I shall not have tasted death.*

Where are the lips that prattled infant lays?
The eyes that shone with light of childhood's days?
The heart that bubbled o'er with boyhood's glee?
The limbs that bounded as the chamois free?
The ears that heard life's music everywhere?
These, all, where are they now? Declare!

Forever gone; forever dead. Yet still
I live. My love, my hate, my fears, my will,

My all that makes life living firm abides.
Dead is my youth, and *so my age must die;*
But I remain—imperishable I.

Speed day and year. Fleet by the streams of time!
Wing, birds of passage, to a sunnier clime.
Come change, come dissolution and decay,
To kill the very semblance of this clay.
Yet, know the conscious, *the unchanging I,*
Through all eternity shall never die.[45]

Such is life! We are brought near persons we love or who
do us good for a time; and then they part from us, or we
are parted from them. We gain friends, and lose them; out
of sight; we have blessings and forfeit them; *all is change;*
. . . and all this *to teach us,* amid all which changes, *to trust
alone in Him who changeth not;* to use faithfully all He
gives us.[46]

Let us take to our hearts a lesson—no lesson can braver be—
From the ways of the tapestry weavers on the other side
    of the sea.
Above their heads the pattern hangs, they study it with
    care,
And while their fingers deftly work, their eyes are fastened
    there.
They tell this curious thing, besides, of a patient, plodding
    weaver;
He wove on the wrong side evermore, but works for the
    right side ever.
It is only when the weaving stops, and the web is tossed
    and turned,
And he sees his real handiwork, that his marvelous skill is
    learned.

Ah, the sight of its delicate beauty, how it pays him for all
it cost,
No rarer, daintier work than his was ever done by the frost.
Thus the master bringeth him golden hire and giveth him
praises as well,
And how happy the heart of the weaver is, no tongue but
his own can tell.
The years of man are the looms of God let down from the
place of the sun,
Wherein we are weaving always, till the mystic web is done.
Weaving kindly; but weaving surely, *each* for himself, *his
fate,*
We may not see how the right side looks, *we can only weave
and wait.*
But *looking above for the pattern,* no weaver hath need to
fear,
Only let him look clear into heaven—the perfect pattern is
there.
If he keeps the face of the Saviour forever and always in
sight,
His toil shall be sweeter than honey, *his weaving is sure to
be right.*
And when his task is ended, and the web is turned and
shown,
He shall hear the voice of the Master, it shall say to him,
"Well done!"
And the white-winged angels of heaven to bear him thence
shall come down,
And God shall give him gold for his hire, not coin, but a
fadeless crown.[47]

Be thou faithful unto death, and I will give thee a crown
of life.[48]

How many there are who fail to realize that the measure of gifts lies not in their size or splendor but in the spirit of their giving!

THE STORY OF THE OTHER WISE MAN

The three wise men followed the star of Bethlehem and found the king. The fourth wise man sold all his possessions that he, too, might bring worthy gifts for the Christ-child. In his girdle he carried the sapphire, the ruby, the pearl, But he was delayed—would he ever reach the King?

After Artaban had been delayed on the journey by the sickness of a Hebrew peasant, he rode fast across the plain only to find the three magi had gone on before. So he must return to Babylon, sell his sapphire, and provide camels to cross the desert. At last he arrived at Bethlehem.

The streets of the village Bethlehem seemed to be deserted, and Artaban wondered whether the men had all gone up to the hill-pastures to bring down their sheep. From the open door of a low stone cottage he heard the sound of a woman's voice singing softly. He entered and found a young mother hushing her baby to rest. She told him of days ago, and how a star had guided them to the place where Joseph of Nazareth was lodging with his wife and her new-born child, and how they had paid reverence to the child, and given him many gifts, and she ended by saying, "The man of Nazareth took the babe and his mother and fled away that same night secretly, and it is whispered that they were going far away to Egypt."

Artaban listened to her gentle, timid speech, and the child in her arms looked up in his face and smiled, stretching out its rosy hands to grasp at the winged circle of gold on his breast.

He spoke, "And so it has not seemed good to the God of

wisdom to reward my search so soon and so easily. The one who I seek has gone before me; and now I must follow the King to Egypt."

The young mother laid the babe in its cradle, and rose to minister to the wants of the stranger guest that fate had brought into her house. She set food before him, the plain fare of the peasants. Artaban accepted it gratefully; and, as he ate, the child fell into a happy slumber, and murmured sweetly in its dreams, and a great peace filled the quiet room.

But suddenly there came the noise of a wild confusion and uproar in the streets of the village, a shrieking and wailing of women's voices, and a clangor of brazen trumpets and a clashing of swords, and a desperate cry; "The soldiers, the soldiers of Herod! They are killing our children."

The young mother's face grew white with terror. She clasped her child to her bosom, and crouched motionless in the darkest corner of the room, covering him with the folds of her robe, lest he should wake and cry.

But Artaban went quickly and stood in the doorway of the house. His broad shoulders filled the portals from side to side, and the peak of the white cap all but reached the lintel.

The soldiers came hurrying down the street with bloody hands and dripping swords. At the sight of the stranger in his imposing dress they hesitated with surprise. The captain of the band approached the threshold to thrust him aside. But Artaban did not stir. His face was as calm as though he were watching the stars, and in his eyes there burned a steady radiance. He held the soldier silently for an instant, and then said in a low voice;

"I am alone in this place, and I am waiting to give this jewel to the prudent captain who will leave me in peace."

He showed the ruby, glistening in the hollow of his hand like a great drop of blood.

The captain was amazed at the splendor of the gem. The pupils of his eyes expanded with desire, and the hard lines of greed wrinkled around his lips. He stretched out his hand and took the ruby.

"March on!" he cried to his men, "There is no child here. The house is still."

The clamor and clang of arms passed down the street. Artaban reentered the cottage. He turned his face to the east and prayed:

"God of truth, forgive my sin." I have said the thing that is not, saved the life of a child. And two of my gifts are gone. *I have spent for man that which was meant for God. Shall I ever be worthy to see the face of the King?"*

"Because thou has saved the life of my little one, may the Lord bless thee and keep thee; the Lord make his face to shine upon thee and be gracious unto thee; The Lord lift up His countenance upon thee and give thee peace," prayed the mother.

* * *

And then in the swiftly passing years Artaban was moving among the throngs of men in the populous Egypt, seeking everywhere for traces of the household that had come down from Bethlehem.

He stood at the foot of the pyramids, which lifted their sharp points into the intense saffron glow of the sunset sky. He looked up into the vast countenance of the crouching Sphinx and vainly tried to read the meaning of the calm eyes and smiling mouth. Was it, indeed, the mockery of all effort and all aspiration?

Artaban was sitting in an obscure house of Alexandria, taking counsel with a Hebrew rabbi. The venerable man, bending over the rolls of parchment said, "And remember my son, the King whom you are seeking is not to be found in a palace, nor among the rich and powerful. This I know. Those who seek Him will do well to look among the poor and the lowly, the sorrowful and the oppressed."

The other wise man could be seen again and again traveling from place to place, *and searching among the people of the* dispersion, with whom the little family from Bethlehem might, perhaps, have found a refuge. *He passed* through countries *where famine lay* heavy upon the land, and the poor were crying for bread. *He made his dwelling in plague-stricken cities* where the sick were languishing in the bitter companionship of the helpless misery. *He visited the oppressed and the afflicted* in the gloom of subterranean prisons, and the crowded wretchedness of slave-markets, and weary toil of galleyships. In all this populous and intricate world of anguish, though he *found none to worship, he found many to help. He fed the hungry,* and clothed the naked, *and healed the sick,* and comforted the captive; and his years went by more swiftly than the weavers shuttle that flashed back and forth through the loom while the web grows and the invisible pattern is completed.

It seemed almost as if he had forgotten his quest. But once he stood alone at sunrise, waiting at the gate of a Roman prison. He had taken from a secret resting-place in his bosom the pearl, *the last of his jewels.* As he looked at it, a mellow lustre, a soft and glowing light, full of shifting gleams of azure and rose, trembled upon its surface. *It seemed almost to have absorbed some reflection of the colors of the lost sapphire and ruby.*

* * *

Three-and-thirty years of the life of Artaban had passed away, and he was still a pilgrim, and a seeker after light. His hair, once darker than the cliffs of Zagros, was now white as the wintry snow that covered them. His eyes, that once flashed like flames of fires were dull as embers smouldering among the ashes.

Worn and weary and ready to die, but *still looking for the King* he had come for the last time to Jerusalem. He had often visited the holy city before, and had searched through all its lanes and crowded hovels and black prisons without finding any trace of the family of Nazarenes who had fled from Bethlehem long ago. But now it seemed as if he must make one more effort, and something whispered in his heart that, at last, he might succeed.

It was the season of the Passover. The city was thronged with strangers. The children of Israel, scattered in far lands, had returned to the Temple for the great feast, and there had been a confusion of tongues in the streets for many days.

But on this day there was singular agitation visible in the multitude. The sky was veiled with a portentous gloom, and currents of excitement seemed to flash through the crowd like the thrill which shakes the forest on the eve of a storm. A secret tide was sweeping them all one way. The clatter of sandals, and the soft, thick sound of thousands of bare feet shuffling over the stones, flowed unceasingly along the street that leads to the Damascus gate.

Artaban joined company with a group of people from his own country, Parthian Jews who had come up to keep the Passover, and inquired of them the cause of the tumult, and where they were going.

"We are going," they answered, "to the palace called Golgotha. Jesus of Nazareth is a man who has done many wonderful works among the people, so that they love him greatly. But the priests and elders have said that he must die, because he gave himself out to be the Son of God, and Pilate has sent him to the cross because he said that he was the 'King of the Jews.'"

How strangely these familiar words fell upon the tired

heart of Artaban! They had led him for a lifetime over land and sea. And now they came to him darkly and mysteriously like a message of despair. The King had arisen, but He had been denied and cast out. He was about to perish. Perhaps He was dying already. Could it be the same who had been born in Bethlehem thirty-three years ago, at whose birth the star had appeared in heaven, and of whose coming the prophets had spoken?

Artaban's heart beat unsteadily. "It may be that I shall find the King, at last, in the hands of His enemies, and shall come in time to offer my pearl for his ransom before He dies."

So the old man followed the multitudes with slow and painful steps toward the Damascus gate of the city. Just beyond the entrance of the guardhouse a troop of Macedonian soldiers came down the street, dragging a young girl with torn dress and dishevelled hair. As the Magian paused to look at her with compassion, she broke suddenly from the hands of her tormentors, and threw herself at his feet, clasping him around the knees. She had seen his white cap and winged circle on his breast.

"Have pity on me," she cried, "and save me, for the sake of the God of Purity! I also am a Daughter of the true religion which is taught of the Magi. My father was a merchant of Parthia, but he is dead, and I am seized for his debts to be sold as a slave. Save me from worse than death."

Artaban trembled.

It was the old conflict in his soul—the conflict between the expectation of faith and the impulse of love. Twice the gift which he had consecrated to the worship of religion had been drawn from his hand to the service of humanity. This was the third trial, the ultimate probation, the *final irrevocable choice.*

Was it his great opportunity, or his last temptation? He

could not tell. One thing only was clear in the darkness of his mind—it was inevitable. And does not the inevitable come from God?

One thing only was sure to his divided heart—to rescue this helpless girl would be a true deed of love. *And is not love the light of the soul?*

He took the pearl from his bosom. *Never had it seemed so luminous, so radiant,* so full of tender, living lustre. He laid it in the hand of the slave.

"This is thy ransom, daughter! *It is the last of my treasures which I kept for the King.*"

While he spoke, the darkness of the sky thickened, and shuddering tremors ran through the earth.

The walls of the houses rocked to and fro. Stones loosened and crashed to the street. Dust clouds filled the air. The soldiers fled in terror, reeling like drunken men. But Artaban and the girl whom he had ransomed crouched helpless beneath the wall of the Praetorium.

What had he to fear? What had he to live for? *He had given away the last remnant of his tribute for the King. The quest was over* and it had failed.

A heavy tile, shaken from the roof, fell and struck the old man on the temple. He lay breathless and pale, with his gray head resting on the young girl's shoulder, and the blood trickling from the wound. As she bent over him, fearing that he was dead, there came a voice through the twilight, very small and still, like the music sounding from a distance, in which the notes are clear but the words are lost. The girl turned to see if some one had spoken from the window above them, but she saw no one.

The old Man's lips began to move, as if in answer, and she heard him say in Parthian tongue:

"Not so, my Lord; For when saw I thee anhungered and fed thee? or thirsty, and gave thee drink? *When saw I thee*

a stranger, and took thee in? Or naked, and clothed thee?
When saw I thee sick or in prison, and came unto thee?
Thirty-and-three years have *I looked for thee; but I have
never seen thy face,* nor ministered to thee my King."

He ceased, and the sweet voice came again. And again the
maid heard it, very faintly and far away. But now it seemed
as though she understood the words:

*"Verily I say unto thee, in as much as thou has done it
unto one of the least of these my brethren, thou has done
it unto me."*

A calm radiance of wonder and joy lighted the pale face
of Artaban like the first ray of dawn on a snowy mountain-
peak. One long last breath of relief gently from his lips.

His journey was ended. *His treasures were accepted. The
Other Wise Man had found the King.*[49]

Religion

> A fire-mist and a planet,
>   A crystal and a cell,
> A jelly-fish and a saurian,
>   And caves where the cave-men dwell;
> Then a sense of law and beauty
>   And a face turned from the clod—
> *Some call it evolution,* ·
>   And *others call it God.*
>
> A haze on the far horizon,
>   The infinite, tender sky,
> The ripe rich tint of the cornfield,
>   And the wild geese sailing high—
> And all over upland and lowland
>   The charm of the golden-rod—
> *Some* of us *call it autumn*
>   And *others call it God.*

Like tides on a crescent sea-beach,
    When the moon is new and thin,
Into our hearts high yearnings
    Come welling and surging in—
Come from the mystic ocean,
    Whose rim no foot has trod,—
Some of us *call it longing,*
    And *others call it God.*

A picket frozen on duty,
    A mother starved for her brood,
Socrates drinking the hemlock,
    And Jesus on the rood;
And millions who, humble and nameless,
    The straight, hard pathway plod,—
Some call it *consecration,*
    And *others call it God.*[50]

We can get in touch with God (through Brotherhood).

"All are but parts of one stupendous whole."[1]

"He who serves his brother best
   Gets nearer God than all the rest."[2]

God, *what a world, if men* in street and mart
Felt that same kinship of the human heart
Which makes them, in the face of *fire* and *flood,*
Rise to the meaning of True Brotherhood.[3]

The quality of mercy is not strained;
It droppeth, as the gentle rain from heaven
Upon the place beneath: it is *twice blessed;*
It blesseth *him that gives,* and *him that takes.*[4]

So live that when thy summons comes to join
The innumerable caravan, that moves
To the pale realms of shade, where each shall take
His chamber in the silent halls of death,
Thou go not like the quarry slave at night
Scourged to his dungeon; but, sustained and soothed
By an unfaltering trust, approach thy grave,
Like one who wraps the drapery of his couch about
   him, and lies down to pleasant dreams.[5]

THE CREST AND CROWNING OF ALL GOOD, LIFE'S FINAL STAR, IS BROTHERHOOD:

For it will bring again to earth
Her long-lost Poesy and Mirth;
Will send new light on every face,
A kingly power upon the race.
And till it comes, we men are slaves,
And travel downward to the dust of graves,
Come, clear the way, then, clear the way:
Blind creeds and kings have had their day.
Break the dead branches from the path:
Our hope is in the aftermath—
Our hope is in heroic men,
Star-led to build the world again.
To this event the ages ran:
Make way for Brotherhood—make way for man![6]

If Jesus should tramp the streets tonight,
    Storm-beaten and hungry for bread,
Seeking a room and a candle light
    And a clean, though humble, bed,
Who would welcome the workman in,
    Though he came with panting breath,
His hands all bruised and his garments thin—
    This workman from Nazareth?

Would rich folk hurry to bind his bruise
    And shelter his stricken form?
Would they *take God in with his muddy shoes*
    Out of the pitiless storm?
Are they not too busy wreathing their flowers
    Or heaping their golden store—
Too busy chasing the bubble hours
    For the poor man's God at the door?

And *if he should come* where *churchmen bow,*
   Forgetting the greater sin,
Would he pause with a light on his wounded brow,
   Would he turn and enter in?
. *And what would he think of their creeds* so dim,
   Of the weak, uplifted hands,
Of their selfish prayers going up to him
   Out of a thousand lands?[7]

Putting God in the Nation's life,
   Bringing us back to the ideal thing—
There's something fine in a creed like that,
   Something true in those words that ring.
Sneer as you will at the "preacher air,"
   Scoff as you will at the Bible tang,
It's putting God in the Nation's life
   That will keep it clear of the crooked "gang".

We've kept Him out of its life too long,
   *We've been afraid—*to our utter shame—
To put Him into our speech and song,
   To stand on the hustings and *speak His name.*
We've put all things in that life but Him,
   We've put our selfishness, pride and show;
It is time for the true ideal to come,
   And time for the low desire to go.

Putting God in the Nation's life,
   Helping us think of the higher things
That is the kind of speech to make
   That is the kind of song to sing.
Upward and forward and let us try,
   The new deal in the forthright way—
Putting God in the Nation's life,
   And putting it there in a style to stay.[8]

O *God*, within whose sight
All men have equal right
   To worship Thee,
Break every bar that holds
Thy flock *in diverse folds;*
Thy will from none withholds
   Full liberty.

Lord, *set Thy churches free*
From foolish rivalry!
   Lord, make all free!
Let all past bitterness
Now and forever cease,
And all our souls possess
   True charity.[9]

Forgive, O Lord, our severing ways,
The rival altars that we raise,
The wrangling tongues that mar thy praise![10]

In Christ there is no East nor West,
   In him no South nor North,
But one great Fellowship of Love
   Throughout the whole wide earth.

In Him shall true hearts everywhere
   Their high communion find,
His service is the golden cord,
   Close-binding all mankind.

Join hands then, brothers of the faith,
   Whate'er your race may be,—
Who serves my Father as a son,
   Is surely *kin to me*.

In Christ now meet both East and West,
  In Him meet South and North,
All Christly souls are one in Him.
  Throughout the whole wide earth.[11]

  All your strength is in your *union,*
  All your *danger is in discord.*
  Therefore be at peace henceforward,
  And as brothers live together.[12]

The first great silence in the life of Jesus holds all His years of growth. It meant study in the shadows of the synagogue, meditation on the upland pastures, prayer beneath the evening stars. The first great silence for every life should be, know thyself. God has given *to* every *individual* soul some gift that is unique, peculiar to itself; *some delicate tint* that it alone can add to the great picture; *some tone that* no other soul can sound forth.[13]

  Prayer, if it be such deep desire
    For good that it shall realize
  Its hope in action, *may aspire*
    To answer, and *not otherwise.*
  So spake the voice *and prayer became*
  A force, no more an emptied name.
  No mere petition could express
  That inward prayer of righteousness
  Nor any supplicating word
  Voice the diviner speech unheard;
  For life itself was made the only prayer
    And life itself the only answer gained;
  Unlimited the soul's expression there
    Unlimited the heart's desire attained.

The eager *stem shall find* its hour
Of *answer in the opened flower,*
And the flower's rapt unfolding lead
To rich *fulfilment in the seed;*
Man's self-dependent *will* to be
In tune with God's *high harmony,*
Right *thinking* ever *turned to act,*
Shall make unceasing *prayer a fact,*
And prayer, thus answered shall allow
A larger faith, and teach it how
To *find its heaven here and now!*[14]

IT IS QUITE SIMPLE *and always will be:*

Why are the saints, saints? Because they were *cheerful,*
when it was difficult to be cheerful, *patient, when it was*
difficult to be patient; and because *they pushed* on when they
wanted to stand still, and kept silent when they wanted to
talk, and were *agreeable when* they *wanted to be disagree-*
able. That was all.[15]

I said, "Let us walk in the fields,"
He said, "No, walk in the town."
I said, "There are no flowers there."
He said, *"No flowers, but a crown."*
I said, "But the skies are black,
There is nothing but noise and din."
And he wept as he sent me back,
"There is more," he said, "there is sin."
I said, "But the air is thick,
And fogs are veiling the sun."
He answered, "Yet hearts are sick,
And souls in the dark undone."
I said, "I shall miss the light,

And friends will miss me, they say."
He answered, *Choose to-night*
If I am to miss you or THEY."
. *I pleaded for time* to be given.
He said, "Is it hard to decide?
It will not seem hard in heaven,
To have followed the steps of your guide."[16]

Earth gets its price for what Earth gives us:
    The beggar is taxed for a corner to die in,
The priest hath his fee who comes and shrives us,
    We bargain for the graves we lie in;
At the devil's booth are all things sold,
    Each ounce of dross costs its ounce of gold:
For a cap and bells our lives we pay,
    Bubbles we buy with a whole soul's tasking:
'Tis heaven alone that is given away,
    'Tis only God may be had for the asking;
No price is set on the lavish summer;
    June may be had by the poorest comer.

                *   *   *

The Holy Supper is kept, indeed,
    In whatso we share with another's need;
Not what we give, but what we share,
    For the gift without the giver is bare;
Who gives himself with his alms *feeds three,*
    Himself, his hungering neighbor, and me.[17]

   What if you should suddenly realize that Christ had been
living in your home for the past five years? What searching
would you give your mind and actions and thoughts? Would
it fill you with fear? Would it bring consolation to you to
know that he had seen your vexations and the way in which
you had accepted them?[18]

The soul of Jesus is restless today;
Christ is tramping through the spirit-world
Compassion in his heart for the fainting millions;
He trudges through China, through Poland,
Through Russia, Austria, Germany, Armenia;
Patiently he pleads with the Church,
Tenderly he woos her.
The wounds of his body are bleeding afresh for the
    sorrows of his shepherdless people.
We besiege him with selfish petitions,
We weary him with our petty ambitions,
From the needy we bury him in piles of carven stone,
We obscure him in the smoke of stuffy incense,
We drown his voice with the snarls and shrieks of our
    disgruntled bickerings,
We build temples to him with hands that are bloody,
We deny him in the needs and sorrows of the exploited
    "least of his brethren".
The soul of Jesus is restless today
But eternally undismayed.[19]

REFLECTION

Religion includes all good, beauty, love, truth, universal
law and all life. We can learn religion not only from the
Bible, but also from nature, inspired poetry, inspired music,
work, and through our service for others. All of the ideas
developed in the preceding chapters are a part of religion.
Right thinking, cheerfulness, appreciation of beauty in na-
ture, love of friends and humanity, knowledge of the rela-
tionship of things to each other and to the universe, under-
standing the purpose of sorrow and accepting it, all help us
to find God.
    Doing outwardly some "recognized religious duty" is not

the only way to be in communion with the Creator. Sacrificing self for another's benefit, caring for a baby, caring for the sick, doing whatever is one's duty is doing God's will. Such a man lives forever in the continued action of the forces he helped to start. Many find a close union with God through nature. He is found every place, and in all good, wherever you look for Him and at all times, "closer is He than breathing and nearer than hands and feet," but found always in the depths of your own heart. "I am with you always!" Peace, contentment, happiness, all things good are from Him. Without Him there is no peace or contentment. Seek and Ye shall find. Knock and the door shall be opened. Free to all! The only free thing in all the world, and the only real thing worth having! Even a flower needs help from another power—the sun. Then do we not need help from another world? Christ did not leave. Christ is still here in spirit today. He was freed from physical limitation, that he might fuse himself into our thoughts, our actions, our lives. Easter is like a plant. In death one merely pushes forth out of this material realm as a plant pushes forth from its clod of clay to become a profusion of unlimited loveliness in a new birth here but in another world. It can be seen in part when sufficiently in harmony with it. Do you recognize Christ when you see Him? He works through us.

Individual Spiritual experiences in Life follow the experiences which Christ went through. Easter can be had only if we earn it, and pay for it, in the coin Christ paid for it. Through His help the mystic chasm between death and eternal life is crossed—that place which none can cross alone.

Our strength cometh from the Lord. By ourselves, we are inanimate, poor things, pitifully dependent for our very existence upon a higher source. Strength comes from love. Is it not true that in proportion to the amount of our love we *have strength to accomplish any task? Love never dies! God is love! Thru Christ likeness we shall reach God.*

Christ said:—

"Freely ye have received, freely give! . . . he that en-dureth shall be saved. . . . there is nothing covered, that shall not be revealed; and hid that shall not be known. Fear not them which kill the body, but are not able to kill the soul; but rather fear him which is able to destroy both soul and body in hell. . . . Whosoever therefore shall confess me before men, him will I confess also before my father which is in Heaven. . . . He that loveth father or mother more than me, is not worthy of me; and he that loveth son or daughter more than me is not worthy of me. And he that taketh not his cross, and followeth after me, is not worthy of me. He that findeth his life shall lose it; and he that loseth his life for my sake shall find it.

"Come unto me, all ye that labor and are heavy laden, and I will give you rest. Take my yoke upon you, and learn of me; for I am meek and lowly in heart: and ye shall find rest unto your souls . . . Every kingdom divided against itself is brought to desolation; and every city or house divided against itself shall not stand. . . . He that is not with me is against me; . . . Either make the tree good, and his fruit good; or else make the tree corrupt, and his fruit corrupt; for the tree is known by his fruit. . . . how can ye, being evil, speak good things? for out of the abundance of the heart the mouth speaketh. A good man, out of the good treasure of the heart, bringeth forth good things. . . . Every idle word that men shall speak, they shall give account thereof in the day of judgment . . . For whosoever shall do the will of my father which is in Heaven, the same is my brother, and sister, and mother . . .

"The kingdom of Heaven is like unto leaven, which a

woman took and hid in three measures of meal, till the whole was leavened . . . If any man will come after me, let him deny himself, and take up his cross, and follow me. For what is a man profited, if he shall gain the whole world, and lose his own soul? . . . For the Son of man shall come in the glory of his Father with his angels; and then he shall reward every man according to his works . . . Verily I say unto you, Except ye be converted and become as little children, ye shall not enter into the kingdom of heaven. Whosoever therefore shall humble himself as this little child, the same is greatest in the kingdom of heaven. . . . For where two or three are gathered together in my name, there am I in the midst of them. . . . With God all things are possible. . . .

"Thou shalt love the Lord thy God with all thy heart, and with all thy soul, and with all thy mind. . . . Thou shalt love thy neighbor as thyself. On these two commandments hang all the Law and the Prophets . . . Therefore be ye also ready; for in such an hour as ye think not the Son of man cometh. . . . Then shall the King say unto them on his right hand, Come, ye blessed of my Father, inherit the kingdom prepared for you from the foundation of the world. . . . Verily I say unto you, inasmuch as ye have done it unto one of the least of these my brethren, ye have done it unto me. . . . Verily I say unto you, Inasmuch as ye did it not to one of the least of these, ye did it not to me. And these shall go away into everlasting punishment: but the righteous into life eternal.

"I know thy works, that thou art neither cold nor hot: I would thou were cold or hot. So then because thou art luke warm, and neither cold nor hot, I will spue thee out of my mouth. . . . As many as I love, I rebuke and chasten; be zealous therefore, and repent. Behold, I stand at the door and knock: if any man hear my voice, and open the door, I

will come unto him, and will sup with him, and he with me.
. . . And, behold, I come quickly; and my reward is with
me, to give every man according as his work shall be. I am
Alpha and Omega, the beginning and the end, the first and
the last.

"Let not your heart be troubled; ye believe in God, believe also in me. I go to prepare a place for you. And, lo, I
am with you always, even unto the end of the world. I am
the way, and the truth, and the life; no man cometh to the
Father, but by me. Take up thy cross and FOLLOW ME!
If ye love me, keep my commandments. . . . Yet a little
while, and the world seeth me no more; but ye see me,
because I live, ye shall live also. . . . But the Comforter,
which is the Holy Ghost, whom the Father will send in
my name, he shall teach you all things. . . . Peace I leave
with you, my peace I give unto you; not as the world
giveth, give I unto you. Let not your heart be troubled,
neither let it be afraid, only believe!"[20]

*As you come to the end of this book, it is the prayer of the
author that you can say:—*

> Softly I closed the book as in a dream
> And let its echoes linger to redeem
> Silence with music, darkness with its gleam.
>
> That day I worked no more I could not bring
> My hands to toil, my thoughts to trafficking,
> A new light shone on every common thing.
>
> Celestial glories flamed before my gaze,
> That day I worked no more, but to God's praise,
> I shall work better all my other days.[21]

INDEX

Many of these selections are from larger original works. For the whole poem see other sources.

CPSIA information can be obtained
at www.ICGtesting.com
Printed in the USA
LVHW021518090222
710691LV00022B/298

9 781014 646392